ISBN 0-8373-2405-X

C-2405 CAREER EXAMINATION SERIES

This is your PASSBOOK® for...

Principal Auditor

Test Preparation Study Guide

Questions & Answers

NLC

NATIONAL LEARNING CORPORATION

National Learning Corporation

212 Michael Drive, Syosset, New York 11791

(516) 921-8888
(800) 645-6337
FAX: (516) 921-8743
www.passbooks.com
sales @ passbooks.com
info @ passbooks.com

PRINTED IN THE UNITED STATES OF AMERICA

PASSBOOK®

NOTICE

This book is SOLELY intended for, is sold ONLY to, and its use is RESTRICTED to *individual*, bona fide applicants or candidates who qualify by virtue of having seriously filed applications for appropriate license, certificate, professional and/or promotional advancement, higher school matriculation, scholarship, or other legitimate requirements of educational and/or governmental authorities.

This book is NOT intended for use, class instruction, tutoring, training, duplication, copying, reprinting, excerption, or adaptation, etc., by:

(1) Other publishers

(2) Proprietors and/or Instructors of "Coaching" and/or Preparatory Courses

(3) Personnel and/or Training Divisions of commercial, industrial, and governmental organizations

(4) Schools, colleges, or universities and/or their departments and staffs, including teachers and other personnel

(5) Testing Agencies or Bureaus

(6) Study groups which seek by the purchase of a single volume to copy and/or duplicate and/or adapt this material for use by the group as a whole without having purchased individual volumes for each of the members of the group

(7) Et al.

Such persons would be in violation of appropriate Federal and State statutes.

PROVISION OF LICENSING AGREEMENTS. — Recognized educational commercial, industrial, and governmental institutions and organizations, and others legitimately engaged in educational pursuits, including training, testing, and measurement activities, may address a request for a licensing agreement to the copyright owners, who will determine whether, and under what conditions, including fees and charges, the materials in this book may be used by them. In other words, a licensing facility exists for the legitimate use of the material in this book on other than an individual basis. However, it is asseverated and affirmed here that the material in this book *CANNOT* be used without the receipt of the express permission of such a licensing agreement from the Publishers.

NATIONAL LEARNING CORPORATION
212 Michael Drive
Syosset, New York 11791

Inquiries re licensing agreements should be addressed to:
The President
National Learning Corporation
212 Michael Drive
Syosset, New York 11791

PASSBOOK SERIES®

THE *PASSBOOK SERIES®* has been created to prepare applicants and candidates for the ultimate academic battlefield – the examination room.

At some time in our lives, each and every one of us may be required to take an examination – for validation, matriculation, admission, qualification, registration, certification, or licensure.

Based on the assumption that every applicant or candidate has met the basic formal educational standards, has taken the required number of courses, and read the necessary texts, the *PASSBOOK SERIES®* furnishes the one special preparation which may assure passing with confidence, instead of failing with insecurity. Examination questions – together with answers – are furnished as the basic vehicle for study so that the mysteries of the examination and its compounding difficulties may be eliminated or diminished by a sure method.

This book is meant to help you pass your examination provided that you qualify and are serious in your objective.

The entire field is reviewed through the huge store of content information which is succinctly presented through a provocative and challenging approach – the question-and-answer method.

A climate of success is established by furnishing the correct answers at the end of each test.

You soon learn to recognize types of questions, forms of questions, and patterns of questioning. You may even begin to anticipate expected outcomes.

You perceive that many questions are repeated or adapted so that you can gain acute insights, which may enable you to score many sure points.

You learn how to confront new questions, or types of questions, and to attack them confidently and work out the correct answers.

You note objectives and emphases, and recognize pitfalls and dangers, so that you may make positive educational adjustments.

Moreover, you are kept fully informed in relation to new concepts, methods, practices, and directions in the field.

You discover that you are actually taking the examination all the time: you are preparing for the examination by "taking" an examination, not by reading extraneous and/or supererogatory textbooks.

In short, this PASSBOOK®, used directedly, should be an important factor in helping you to pass your test.

PRINCIPAL AUDITOR

DUTIES

An employee in this class supervises professional personnel in auditing the financial records of one or more of the departments or contractors of the county government. Work may include development of accounting procedures and techniques designed to meet specialized department needs. The incumbent schedules audit assignments and reviews auditing reports submitted by personnel for adherence to established auditing principles, policies and procedures. Performs related work as required.

SCOPE OF THE EXAMINATION

The written test will cover knowledge, skills, and/or abilities in such areas as:

1. Administrative supervision;
2. General accounting;
3. General auditing;
4. Governmental accounting;
5. Preparing written material;
6. Understanding and interpreting tabular material.

HOW TO TAKE A TEST

I. YOU MUST PASS AN EXAMINATION

A. WHAT EVERY CANDIDATE SHOULD KNOW

Examination applicants often ask us for help in preparing for the written test. What can I study in advance? What kinds of questions will be asked? How will the test be given? How will the papers be graded?

As an applicant for a civil service examination, you may be wondering about some of these things. Our purpose here is to suggest effective methods of advance study and to describe civil service examinations.

Your chances for success on this examination can be increased if you know how to prepare. Those "pre-examination jitters" can be reduced if you know what to expect. You can even experience an adventure in good citizenship if you know why civil service exams are given.

B. WHY ARE CIVIL SERVICE EXAMINATIONS GIVEN?

Civil service examinations are important to you in two ways. As a citizen, you want public jobs filled by employees who know how to do their work. As a job seeker, you want a fair chance to compete for that job on an equal footing with other candidates. The best-known means of accomplishing this two-fold goal is the competitive examination.

Exams are widely publicized throughout the nation. They may be administered for jobs in federal, state, city, municipal, town or village governments or agencies.

Any citizen may apply, with some limitations, such as the age or residence of applicants. Your experience and education may be reviewed to see whether you meet the requirements for the particular examination. When these requirements exist, they are reasonable and applied consistently to all applicants. Thus, a competitive examination may cause you some uneasiness now, but it is your privilege and safeguard.

C. HOW ARE CIVIL SERVICE EXAMS DEVELOPED?

Examinations are carefully written by trained technicians who are specialists in the field known as "psychological measurement," in consultation with recognized authorities in the field of work that the test will cover. These experts recommend the subject matter areas or skills to be tested; only those knowledges or skills important to your success on the job are included. The most reliable books and source materials available are used as references. Together, the experts and technicians judge the difficulty level of the questions.

Test technicians know how to phrase questions so that the problem is clearly stated. Their ethics do not permit "trick" or "catch" questions. Questions may have been tried out on sample groups, or subjected to statistical analysis, to determine their usefulness.

Written tests are often used in combination with performance tests, ratings of training and experience, and oral interviews. All of these measures combine to form the best-known means of finding the right person for the right job.

II. HOW TO PASS THE WRITTEN TEST

A. NATURE OF THE EXAMINATION

To prepare intelligently for civil service examinations, you should know how they differ from school examinations you have taken. In school you were assigned certain definite pages to read or subjects to cover. The examination questions were quite detailed and usually emphasized memory. Civil service exams, on the other hand, try to discover your present ability to perform the duties of a position, plus your potentiality to learn these duties. In other words, a civil service exam attempts to predict how successful you will be. Questions cover such a broad area that they cannot be as minute and detailed as school exam questions.

In the public service similar kinds of work, or positions, are grouped together in one "class." This process is known as *position-classification.* All the positions in a class are paid according to the salary range for that class. One class title covers all of these positions, and they are all tested by the same examination.

B. FOUR BASIC STEPS

1) Study the announcement

How, then, can you know what subjects to study? Our best answer is: "Learn as much as possible about the class of positions for which you've applied." The exam will test the knowledge, skills and abilities needed to do the work.

Your most valuable source of information about the position you want is the official exam announcement. This announcement lists the training and experience qualifications. Check these standards and apply only if you come reasonably close to meeting them.

The brief description of the position in the examination announcement offers some clues to the subjects which will be tested. Think about the job itself. Review the duties in your mind. Can you perform them, or are there some in which you are rusty? Fill in the blank spots in your preparation.

Many jurisdictions preview the written test in the exam announcement by including a section called "Knowledge and Abilities Required," "Scope of the Examination," or some similar heading. Here you will find out specifically what fields will be tested.

2) Review your own background

Once you learn in general what the position is all about, and what you need to know to do the work, ask yourself which subjects you already know fairly well and which need improvement. You may wonder whether to concentrate on improving your strong areas or on building some background in your fields of weakness. When the announcement has specified "some knowledge" or "considerable knowledge," or has used adjectives like "beginning principles of..." or "advanced ... methods," you can get a clue as to the number and difficulty of questions to be asked in any given field. More questions, and hence broader coverage, would be included for those subjects which are more important in the work. Now weigh your strengths and weaknesses against the job requirements and prepare accordingly.

3) Determine the level of the position

Another way to tell how intensively you should prepare is to understand the level of the job for which you are applying. Is it the entering level? In other words, is this the position in which beginners in a field of work are hired? Or is it an intermediate or advanced level? Sometimes this is indicated by such words as "Junior" or "Senior" in the class title. Other jurisdictions use Roman numerals to designate the level – Clerk I, Clerk II, for example. The word "Supervisor" sometimes appears in the title. If the level is not indicated by the title, check the description of duties. Will you be working under very close supervision, or will you have responsibility for independent decisions in this work?

4) Choose appropriate study materials

Now that you know the subjects to be examined and the relative amount of each subject to be covered, you can choose suitable study materials. For beginning level jobs, or even advanced ones, if you have a pronounced weakness in some aspect of your training, read a modern, standard textbook in that field. Be sure it is up to date and has general coverage. Such books are normally available at your library, and the librarian will be glad to help you locate one. For entry-level positions, questions of appropriate difficulty are chosen – neither highly advanced questions, nor those too simple. Such questions require careful thought but not advanced training.

If the position for which you are applying is technical or advanced, you will read more advanced, specialized material. If you are already familiar with the basic principles of your field, elementary textbooks would waste your time. Concentrate on advanced textbooks and technical periodicals. Think through the concepts and review difficult problems in your field.

These are all general sources. You can get more ideas on your own initiative, following these leads. For example, training manuals and publications of the government agency which employs workers in your field can be useful, particularly for technical and professional positions. A letter or visit to the government department involved may result in more specific study suggestions, and certainly will provide you with a more definite idea of the exact nature of the position you are seeking.

III. KINDS OF TESTS

Tests are used for purposes other than measuring knowledge and ability to perform specified duties. For some positions, it is equally important to test ability to make adjustments to new situations or to profit from training. In others, basic mental abilities not dependent on information are essential. Questions which test these things may not appear as pertinent to the duties of the position as those which test for knowledge and information. Yet they are often highly important parts of a fair examination. For very general questions, it is almost impossible to help you direct your study efforts. What we can do is to point out some of the more common of these general abilities needed in public service positions and describe some typical questions.

1) General information

Broad, general information has been found useful for predicting job success in some kinds of work. This is tested in a variety of ways, from vocabulary lists to questions about current events. Basic background in some field of work, such as sociology or economics, may be sampled in a group of questions. Often these are principles which have become familiar to most persons through exposure rather than through formal training. It is difficult to advise you how to study for these questions; being alert to the world around you is our best suggestion.

2) Verbal ability

An example of an ability needed in many positions is verbal or language ability. Verbal ability is, in brief, the ability to use and understand words. Vocabulary and grammar tests are typical measures of this ability. Reading comprehension or paragraph interpretation questions are common in many kinds of civil service tests. You are given a paragraph of written material and asked to find its central meaning.

3) Numerical ability

Number skills can be tested by the familiar arithmetic problem, by checking paired lists of numbers to see which are alike and which are different, or by interpreting charts and graphs. In the latter test, a graph may be printed in the test booklet which you are asked to use as the basis for answering questions.

4) Observation

A popular test for law-enforcement positions is the observation test. A picture is shown to you for several minutes, then taken away. Questions about the picture test your ability to observe both details and larger elements.

5) Following directions

In many positions in the public service, the employee must be able to carry out written instructions dependably and accurately. You may be given a chart with several columns, each column listing a variety of information. The questions require you to carry out directions involving the information given in the chart.

6) Skills and aptitudes

Performance tests effectively measure some manual skills and aptitudes. When the skill is one in which you are trained, such as typing or shorthand, you can practice. These tests are often very much like those given in business school or high school courses. For many of the other skills and aptitudes, however, no short-time preparation can be made. Skills and abilities natural to you or that you have developed throughout your lifetime are being tested.

Many of the general questions just described provide all the data needed to answer the questions and ask you to use your reasoning ability to find the answers. Your best preparation for these tests, as well as for tests of facts and ideas, is to be at your physical and mental best. You, no doubt, have your own methods of getting into an exam-taking mood and keeping "in shape." The next section lists some ideas on this subject.

IV. KINDS OF QUESTIONS

Only rarely is the "essay" question, which you answer in narrative form, used in civil service tests. Civil service tests are usually of the short-answer type. Full instructions for answering these questions will be given to you at the examination. But in case this is your first experience with short-answer questions and separate answer sheets, here is what you need to know:

1) Multiple-choice Questions

Most popular of the short-answer questions is the "multiple choice" or "best answer" question. It can be used, for example, to test for factual knowledge, ability to solve problems or judgment in meeting situations found at work.

A multiple-choice question is normally one of three types—

- It can begin with an incomplete statement followed by several possible endings. You are to find the one ending which *best* completes the statement, although some of the others may not be entirely wrong.
- It can also be a complete statement in the form of a question which is answered by choosing one of the statements listed.
- It can be in the form of a problem – again you select the best answer.

Here is an example of a multiple-choice question with a discussion which should give you some clues as to the method for choosing the right answer:

When an employee has a complaint about his assignment, the action which will *best* help him overcome his difficulty is to

A. discuss his difficulty with his coworkers
B. take the problem to the head of the organization
C. take the problem to the person who gave him the assignment
D. say nothing to anyone about his complaint

In answering this question, you should study each of the choices to find which is best. Consider choice "A" – Certainly an employee may discuss his complaint with fellow employees, but no change or improvement can result, and the complaint remains unresolved. Choice "B" is a poor choice since the head of the organization probably does not know what assignment you have been given, and taking your problem to him is known as "going over the head" of the supervisor. The supervisor, or person who made the assignment, is the person who can clarify it or correct any injustice. Choice "C" is, therefore, correct. To say nothing, as in choice "D," is unwise. Supervisors have and interest in knowing the problems employees are facing, and the employee is seeking a solution to his problem.

2) True/False Questions

The "true/false" or "right/wrong" form of question is sometimes used. Here a complete statement is given. Your job is to decide whether the statement is right or wrong.

SAMPLE: A person-to-person long-distance telephone call costs less than a station-to-station call to the same city.

This statement is wrong, or false, since person-to-person calls are more expensive.

This is not a complete list of all possible question forms, although most of the others are variations of these common types. You will always get complete directions for answering questions. Be sure you understand *how* to mark your answers – ask questions until you do.

V. RECORDING YOUR ANSWERS

For an examination with very few applicants, you may be told to record your answers in the test booklet itself. Separate answer sheets are much more common. If this separate answer sheet is to be scored by machine – and this is often the case – it is highly important that you mark your answers correctly in order to get credit.

An electric scoring machine is often used in civil service offices because of the speed with which papers can be scored. Machine-scored answer sheets must be marked with a pencil, which will be given to you. This pencil has a high graphite content which responds to the electric scoring machine. As a matter of fact, stray dots may register as answers, so do not let your pencil rest on the answer sheet while you are pondering the correct answer. Also, if your pencil lead breaks or is otherwise defective, ask for another.

Since the answer sheet will be dropped in a slot in the scoring machine, be careful not to bend the corners or get the paper crumpled.

The answer sheet normally has five vertical columns of numbers, with 30 numbers to a column. These numbers correspond to the question numbers in your test booklet. After each number, going across the page are four or five pairs of dotted lines. These short dotted lines have small letters or numbers above them. The first two pairs may also have a "T" or "F" above the letters. This indicates that the first two pairs only are to be used if the questions are of the true-false type. If the questions are multiple choice, disregard the "T" and "F" and pay attention only to the small letters or numbers.

Answer your questions in the manner of the sample that follows:

32. The largest city in the United States is
    - A. Washington, D.C.
    - B. New York City
    - C. Chicago
    - D. Detroit
    - E. San Francisco

1) Choose the answer you think is best. (New York City is the largest, so "B" is correct.)
2) Find the row of dotted lines numbered the same as the question you are answering. (Find row number 32)
3) Find the pair of dotted lines corresponding to the answer. (Find the pair of lines under the mark "B.")
4) Make a solid black mark between the dotted lines.

VI. BEFORE THE TEST

Common sense will help you find procedures to follow to get ready for an examination. Too many of us, however, overlook these sensible measures. Indeed, nervousness and fatigue have been found to be the most serious reasons why applicants fail to do their best on civil service tests. Here is a list of reminders:

- Begin your preparation early – Don't wait until the last minute to go scurrying around for books and materials or to find out what the position is all about.
- Prepare continuously – An hour a night for a week is better than an all-night cram session. This has been definitely established. What is more, a night a

week for a month will return better dividends than crowding your study into a shorter period of time.

- Locate the place of the exam – You have been sent a notice telling you when and where to report for the examination. If the location is in a different town or otherwise unfamiliar to you, it would be well to inquire the best route and learn something about the building.
- Relax the night before the test – Allow your mind to rest. Do not study at all that night. Plan some mild recreation or diversion; then go to bed early and get a good night's sleep.
- Get up early enough to make a leisurely trip to the place for the test – This way unforeseen events, traffic snarls, unfamiliar buildings, etc. will not upset you.
- Dress comfortably – A written test is not a fashion show. You will be known by number and not by name, so wear something comfortable.
- Leave excess paraphernalia at home – Shopping bags and odd bundles will get in your way. You need bring only the items mentioned in the official notice you received; usually everything you need is provided. Do not bring reference books to the exam. They will only confuse those last minutes and be taken away from you when in the test room.
- Arrive somewhat ahead of time – If because of transportation schedules you must get there very early, bring a newspaper or magazine to take your mind off yourself while waiting.
- Locate the examination room – When you have found the proper room, you will be directed to the seat or part of the room where you will sit. Sometimes you are given a sheet of instructions to read while you are waiting. Do not fill out any forms until you are told to do so; just read them and be prepared.
- Relax and prepare to listen to the instructions
- If you have any physical problem that may keep you from doing your best, be sure to tell the test administrator. If you are sick or in poor health, you really cannot do your best on the exam. You can come back and take the test some other time.

VII. AT THE TEST

The day of the test is here and you have the test booklet in your hand. The temptation to get going is very strong. Caution! There is more to success than knowing the right answers. You must know how to identify your papers and understand variations in the type of short-answer question used in this particular examination. Follow these suggestions for maximum results from your efforts:

1) Cooperate with the monitor

The test administrator has a duty to create a situation in which you can be as much at ease as possible. He will give instructions, tell you when to begin, check to see that you are marking your answer sheet correctly, and so on. He is not there to guard you, although he will see that your competitors do not take unfair advantage. He wants to help you do your best.

2) Listen to all instructions

Don't jump the gun! Wait until you understand all directions. In most civil service tests you get more time than you need to answer the questions. So don't be in a hurry.

Read each word of instructions until you clearly understand the meaning. Study the examples, listen to all announcements and follow directions. Ask questions if you do not understand what to do.

3) Identify your papers

Civil service exams are usually identified by number only. You will be assigned a number; you must not put your name on your test papers. Be sure to copy your number correctly. Since more than one exam may be given, copy your exact examination title.

4) Plan your time

Unless you are told that a test is a "speed" or "rate of work" test, speed itself is usually not important. Time enough to answer all the questions will be provided, but this does not mean that you have all day. An overall time limit has been set. Divide the total time (in minutes) by the number of questions to determine the approximate time you have for each question.

5) Do not linger over difficult questions

If you come across a difficult question, mark it with a paper clip (useful to have along) and come back to it when you have been through the booklet. One caution if you do this – be sure to skip a number on your answer sheet as well. Check often to be sure that you have not lost your place and that you are marking in the row numbered the same as the question you are answering.

6) Read the questions

Be sure you know what the question asks! Many capable people are unsuccessful because they failed to *read* the questions correctly.

7) Answer all questions

Unless you have been instructed that a penalty will be deducted for incorrect answers, it is better to guess than to omit a question.

8) Speed tests

It is often better NOT to guess on speed tests. It has been found that on timed tests people are tempted to spend the last few seconds before time is called in marking answers at random – without even reading them – in the hope of picking up a few extra points. To discourage this practice, the instructions may warn you that your score will be "corrected" for guessing. That is, a penalty will be applied. The incorrect answers will be deducted from the correct ones, or some other penalty formula will be used.

9) Review your answers

If you finish before time is called, go back to the questions you guessed or omitted to give them further thought. Review other answers if you have time.

10) Return your test materials

If you are ready to leave before others have finished or time is called, take ALL your materials to the monitor and leave quietly. Never take any test material with you. The monitor can discover whose papers are not complete, and taking a test booklet may be grounds for disqualification.

VIII. EXAMINATION TECHNIQUES

1) Read the general instructions carefully. These are usually printed on the first page of the exam booklet. As a rule, these instructions refer to the timing of the examination; the fact that you should not start work until the signal and must stop work at a signal, etc. If there are any *special* instructions, such as a choice of questions to be answered, make sure that you note this instruction carefully.

2) When you are ready to start work on the examination, that is as soon as the signal has been given, read the instructions to each question booklet, underline any key words or phrases, such as *least, best, outline, describe* and the like. In this way you will tend to answer as requested rather than discover on reviewing your paper that you *listed without describing*, that you selected the *worst* choice rather than the *best* choice, etc.

3) If the examination is of the objective or multiple-choice type – that is, each question will also give a series of possible answers: A, B, C or D, and you are called upon to select the best answer and write the letter next to that answer on your answer paper – it is advisable to start answering each question in turn. There may be anywhere from 50 to 100 such questions in the three or four hours allotted and you can see how much time would be taken if you read through all the questions before beginning to answer any. Furthermore, if you come across a question or group of questions which you know would be difficult to answer, it would undoubtedly affect your handling of all the other questions.

4) If the examination is of the essay type and contains but a few questions, it is a moot point as to whether you should read all the questions before starting to answer any one. Of course, if you are given a choice – say five out of seven and the like – then it is essential to read all the questions so you can eliminate the two that are most difficult. If, however, you are asked to answer all the questions, there may be danger in trying to answer the easiest one first because you may find that you will spend too much time on it. The best technique is to answer the first question, then proceed to the second, etc.

5) Time your answers. Before the exam begins, write down the time it started, then add the time allowed for the examination and write down the time it must be completed, then divide the time available somewhat as follows:
   - If 3-1/2 hours are allowed, that would be 210 minutes. If you have 80 objective-type questions, that would be an average of 2-1/2 minutes per question. Allow yourself no more than 2 minutes per question, or a total of 160 minutes, which will permit about 50 minutes to review.
   - If for the time allotment of 210 minutes there are 7 essay questions to answer, that would average about 30 minutes a question. Give yourself only 25 minutes per question so that you have about 35 minutes to review.

6) The most important instruction is to *read each question* and make sure you know what is wanted. The second most important instruction is to *time yourself properly* so that you answer every question. The third most

important instruction is to *answer every question.* Guess if you have to but include something for each question. Remember that you will receive no credit for a blank and will probably receive some credit if you write something in answer to an essay question. If you guess a letter – say "B" for a multiple-choice question – you may have guessed right. If you leave a blank as an answer to a multiple-choice question, the examiners may respect your feelings but it will not add a point to your score. Some exams may penalize you for wrong answers, so in such cases *only,* you may not want to guess unless you have some basis for your answer.

7) Suggestions

a. Objective-type questions

1. Examine the question booklet for proper sequence of pages and questions
2. Read all instructions carefully
3. Skip any question which seems too difficult; return to it after all other questions have been answered
4. Apportion your time properly; do not spend too much time on any single question or group of questions
5. Note and underline key words – *all, most, fewest, least, best, worst, same, opposite,* etc.
6. Pay particular attention to negatives
7. Note unusual option, e.g., unduly long, short, complex, different or similar in content to the body of the question
8. Observe the use of "hedging" words – *probably, may, most likely,* etc.
9. Make sure that your answer is put next to the same number as the question
10. Do not second-guess unless you have good reason to believe the second answer is definitely more correct
11. Cross out original answer if you decide another answer is more accurate; do not erase until you are ready to hand your paper in
12. Answer all questions; guess unless instructed otherwise
13. Leave time for review

b. Essay questions

1. Read each question carefully
2. Determine exactly what is wanted. Underline key words or phrases.
3. Decide on outline or paragraph answer
4. Include many different points and elements unless asked to develop any one or two points or elements
5. Show impartiality by giving pros and cons unless directed to select one side only
6. Make and write down any assumptions you find necessary to answer the questions
7. Watch your English, grammar, punctuation and choice of words
8. Time your answers; don't crowd material

8) Answering the essay question

Most essay questions can be answered by framing the specific response around several key words or ideas. Here are a few such key words or ideas:

M's: manpower, materials, methods, money, management
P's: purpose, program, policy, plan, procedure, practice, problems, pitfalls, personnel, public relations

a. Six basic steps in handling problems:
   1. Preliminary plan and background development
   2. Collect information, data and facts
   3. Analyze and interpret information, data and facts
   4. Analyze and develop solutions as well as make recommendations
   5. Prepare report and sell recommendations
   6. Install recommendations and follow up effectiveness

b. Pitfalls to avoid
   1. *Taking things for granted* – A statement of the situation does not necessarily imply that each of the elements is necessarily true; for example, a complaint may be invalid and biased so that all that can be taken for granted is that a complaint has been registered
   2. *Considering only one side of a situation* – Wherever possible, indicate several alternatives and then point out the reasons you selected the best one
   3. *Failing to indicate follow up* – Whenever your answer indicates action on your part, make certain that you will take proper follow-up action to see how successful your recommendations, procedures or actions turn out to be
   4. *Taking too long in answering any single question* – Remember to time your answers properly

IX. AFTER THE TEST

Scoring procedures differ in detail among civil service jurisdictions although the general principles are the same. Whether the papers are hand-scored or graded by machine we have described, they are nearly always graded by number. That is, the person who marks the paper knows only the number – never the name – of the applicant. Not until all the papers have been graded will they be matched with names. If other tests, such as training and experience or oral interview ratings have been given, scores will be combined. Different parts of the examination usually have different weights. For example, the written test might count 60 percent of the final grade, and a rating of training and experience 40 percent. In many jurisdictions, veterans will have a certain number of points added to their grades.

After the final grade has been determined, the names are placed in grade order and an eligible list is established. There are various methods for resolving ties between those who get the same final grade – probably the most common is to place first the name of the person whose application was received first. Job offers are made from the eligible list in the order the names appear on it. You will be notified of your grade and your rank as soon as all these computations have been made. This will be done as rapidly as possible.

People who are found to meet the requirements in the announcement are called "eligibles." Their names are put on a list of eligible candidates. An eligible's chances of getting a job depend on how high he stands on this list and how fast agencies are filling jobs from the list.

When a job is to be filled from a list of eligibles, the agency asks for the names of people on the list of eligibles for that job. When the civil service commission receives this request, it sends to the agency the names of the three people highest on this list. Or, if the job to be filled has specialized requirements, the office sends the agency the names of the top three persons who meet these requirements from the general list.

The appointing officer makes a choice from among the three people whose names were sent to him. If the selected person accepts the appointment, the names of the others are put back on the list to be considered for future openings.

That is the rule in hiring from all kinds of eligible lists, whether they are for typist, carpenter, chemist, or something else. For every vacancy, the appointing officer has his choice of any one of the top three eligibles on the list. This explains why the person whose name is on top of the list sometimes does not get an appointment when some of the persons lower on the list do. If the appointing officer chooses the second or third eligible, the No. 1 eligible does not get a job at once, but stays on the list until he is appointed or the list is terminated.

X. HOW TO PASS THE INTERVIEW TEST

The examination for which you applied requires an oral interview test. You have already taken the written test and you are now being called for the interview test – the final part of the formal examination.

You may think that it is not possible to prepare for an interview test and that there are no procedures to follow during an interview. Our purpose is to point out some things you can do in advance that will help you and some good rules to follow and pitfalls to avoid while you are being interviewed.

What is an interview supposed to test?

The written examination is designed to test the technical knowledge and competence of the candidate; the oral is designed to evaluate intangible qualities, not readily measured otherwise, and to establish a list showing the relative fitness of each candidate – as measured against his competitors – for the position sought. Scoring is not on the basis of "right" and "wrong," but on a sliding scale of values ranging from "not passable" to "outstanding." As a matter of fact, it is possible to achieve a relatively low score without a single "incorrect" answer because of evident weakness in the qualities being measured.

Occasionally, an examination may consist entirely of an oral test – either an individual or a group oral. In such cases, information is sought concerning the technical knowledges and abilities of the candidate, since there has been no written examination for this purpose. More commonly, however, an oral test is used to supplement a written examination.

Who conducts interviews?

The composition of oral boards varies among different jurisdictions. In nearly all, a representative of the personnel department serves as chairman. One of the members of the board may be a representative of the department in which the candidate would work. In some cases, "outside experts" are used, and, frequently, a businessman or some other representative of the general public is asked to serve. Labor and management or other special groups may be represented. The aim is to secure the services of experts in the appropriate field.

However the board is composed, it is a good idea (and not at all improper or unethical) to ascertain in advance of the interview who the members are and what groups they represent. When you are introduced to them, you will have some idea of their backgrounds and interests, and at least you will not stutter and stammer over their names.

What should be done before the interview?

While knowledge about the board members is useful and takes some of the surprise element out of the interview, there is other preparation which is more substantive. It *is* possible to prepare for an oral interview – in several ways:

1) Keep a copy of your application and review it carefully before the interview

This may be the only document before the oral board, and the starting point of the interview. Know what education and experience you have listed there, and the sequence and dates of all of it. Sometimes the board will ask you to review the highlights of your experience for them; you should not have to hem and haw doing it.

2) Study the class specification and the examination announcement

Usually, the oral board has one or both of these to guide them. The qualities, characteristics or knowledges required by the position sought are stated in these documents. They offer valuable clues as to the nature of the oral interview. For example, if the job involves supervisory responsibilities, the announcement will usually indicate that knowledge of modern supervisory methods and the qualifications of the candidate as a supervisor will be tested. If so, you can expect such questions, frequently in the form of a hypothetical situation which you are expected to solve. NEVER go into an oral without knowledge of the duties and responsibilities of the job you seek.

3) Think through each qualification required

Try to visualize the kind of questions you would ask if you were a board member. How well could you answer them? Try especially to appraise your own knowledge and background in each area, *measured against the job sought*, and identify any areas in which you are weak. Be critical and realistic – do not flatter yourself.

4) Do some general reading in areas in which you feel you may be weak

For example, if the job involves supervision and your past experience has NOT, some general reading in supervisory methods and practices, particularly in the field of human relations, might be useful. Do NOT study agency procedures or detailed manuals. The oral board will be testing your understanding and capacity, not your memory.

5) Get a good night's sleep and watch your general health and mental attitude

You will want a clear head at the interview. Take care of a cold or any other minor ailment, and of course, no hangovers.

What should be done on the day of the interview?

Now comes the day of the interview itself. Give yourself plenty of time to get there. Plan to arrive somewhat ahead of the scheduled time, particularly if your appointment is in the fore part of the day. If a previous candidate fails to appear, the board might be ready for you a bit early. By early afternoon an oral board is almost invariably behind schedule if there are many candidates, and you may have to wait.

Take along a book or magazine to read, or your application to review, but leave any extraneous material in the waiting room when you go in for your interview. In any event, relax and compose yourself.

The matter of dress is important. The board is forming impressions about you – from your experience, your manners, your attitude, and your appearance. Give your personal appearance careful attention. Dress your best, but not your flashiest. Choose conservative, appropriate clothing, and be sure it is immaculate. This is a business interview, and your appearance should indicate that you regard it as such. Besides, being well groomed and properly dressed will help boost your confidence.

Sooner or later, someone will call your name and escort you into the interview room. *This is it.* From here on you are on your own. It is too late for any more preparation. But remember, you asked for this opportunity to prove your fitness, and you are here because your request was granted.

What happens when you go in?

The usual sequence of events will be as follows: The clerk (who is often the board stenographer) will introduce you to the chairman of the oral board, who will introduce you to the other members of the board. Acknowledge the introductions before you sit down. Do not be surprised if you find a microphone facing you or a stenotypist sitting by. Oral interviews are usually recorded in the event of an appeal or other review.

Usually the chairman of the board will open the interview by reviewing the highlights of your education and work experience from your application – primarily for the benefit of the other members of the board, as well as to get the material into the record. Do not interrupt or comment unless there is an error or significant misinterpretation; if that is the case, do not hesitate. But do not quibble about insignificant matters. Also, he will usually ask you some question about your education, experience or your present job – partly to get you to start talking and to establish the interviewing "rapport." He may start the actual questioning, or turn it over to one of the other members. Frequently, each member undertakes the questioning on a particular area, one in which he is perhaps most competent, so you can expect each member to participate in the examination. Because time is limited, you may also expect some rather abrupt switches in the direction the questioning takes, so do not be upset by it. Normally, a board member will not pursue a single line of questioning unless he discovers a particular strength or weakness.

After each member has participated, the chairman will usually ask whether any member has any further questions, then will ask you if you have anything you wish to add. Unless you are expecting this question, it may floor you. Worse, it may start you off on an extended, extemporaneous speech. The board is not usually seeking more information. The question is principally to offer you a last opportunity to present further qualifications or to indicate that you have nothing to add. So, if you feel that a significant qualification or characteristic has been overlooked, it is proper to point it out in a sentence or so. Do not compliment the board on the thoroughness of their examination – they have been sketchy, and you know it. If you wish, merely say, "No thank you, I have nothing further to add." This is a point where you can "talk yourself out" of a good impression or fail to present an important bit of information. Remember, *you close the interview yourself.*

The chairman will then say, "That is all, Mr. _______, thank you." Do not be startled; the interview is over, and quicker than you think. Thank him, gather your belongings and take your leave. Save your sigh of relief for the other side of the door.

How to put your best foot forward

Throughout this entire process, you may feel that the board individually and collectively is trying to pierce your defenses, seek out your hidden weaknesses and embarrass and confuse you. Actually, this is not true. They are obliged to make an appraisal of your qualifications for the job you are seeking, and they want to see you in your best light. Remember, they must interview all candidates and a non-cooperative candidate may become a failure in spite of their best efforts to bring out his qualifications. Here are 15 suggestions that will help you:

1) Be natural – Keep your attitude confident, not cocky

If you are not confident that you can do the job, do not expect the board to be. Do not apologize for your weaknesses, try to bring out your strong points. The board is interested in a positive, not negative, presentation. Cockiness will antagonize any board member and make him wonder if you are covering up a weakness by a false show of strength.

2) Get comfortable, but don't lounge or sprawl

Sit erectly but not stiffly. A careless posture may lead the board to conclude that you are careless in other things, or at least that you are not impressed by the importance of the occasion. Either conclusion is natural, even if incorrect. Do not fuss with your clothing, a pencil or an ashtray. Your hands may occasionally be useful to emphasize a point; do not let them become a point of distraction.

3) Do not wisecrack or make small talk

This is a serious situation, and your attitude should show that you consider it as such. Further, the time of the board is limited – they do not want to waste it, and neither should you.

4) Do not exaggerate your experience or abilities

In the first place, from information in the application or other interviews and sources, the board may know more about you than you think. Secondly, you probably will not get away with it. An experienced board is rather adept at spotting such a situation, so do not take the chance.

5) If you know a board member, do not make a point of it, yet do not hide it

Certainly you are not fooling him, and probably not the other members of the board. Do not try to take advantage of your acquaintanceship – it will probably do you little good.

6) Do not dominate the interview

Let the board do that. They will give you the clues – do not assume that you have to do all the talking. Realize that the board has a number of questions to ask you, and do not try to take up all the interview time by showing off your extensive knowledge of the answer to the first one.

7) Be attentive

You only have 20 minutes or so, and you should keep your attention at its sharpest throughout. When a member is addressing a problem or question to you, give him your undivided attention. Address your reply principally to him, but do not exclude the other board members.

8) Do not interrupt

A board member may be stating a problem for you to analyze. He will ask you a question when the time comes. Let him state the problem, and wait for the question.

9) Make sure you understand the question

Do not try to answer until you are sure what the question is. If it is not clear, restate it in your own words or ask the board member to clarify it for you. However, do not haggle about minor elements.

10) Reply promptly but not hastily

A common entry on oral board rating sheets is "candidate responded readily," or "candidate hesitated in replies." Respond as promptly and quickly as you can, but do not jump to a hasty, ill-considered answer.

11) Do not be peremptory in your answers

A brief answer is proper – but do not fire your answer back. That is a losing game from your point of view. The board member can probably ask questions much faster than you can answer them.

12) Do not try to create the answer you think the board member wants

He is interested in what kind of mind you have and how it works – not in playing games. Furthermore, he can usually spot this practice and will actually grade you down on it.

13) Do not switch sides in your reply merely to agree with a board member

Frequently, a member will take a contrary position merely to draw you out and to see if you are willing and able to defend your point of view. Do not start a debate, yet do not surrender a good position. If a position is worth taking, it is worth defending.

14) Do not be afraid to admit an error in judgment if you are shown to be wrong

The board knows that you are forced to reply without any opportunity for careful consideration. Your answer may be demonstrably wrong. If so, admit it and get on with the interview.

15) Do not dwell at length on your present job

The opening question may relate to your present assignment. Answer the question but do not go into an extended discussion. You are being examined for a *new* job, not your present one. As a matter of fact, try to phrase ALL your answers in terms of the job for which you are being examined.

Basis of Rating

Probably you will forget most of these "do's" and "don'ts" when you walk into the oral interview room. Even remembering them all will not ensure you a passing grade. Perhaps you did not have the qualifications in the first place. But remembering them will help you to put your best foot forward, without treading on the toes of the board members.

Rumor and popular opinion to the contrary notwithstanding, an oral board wants you to make the best appearance possible. They know you are under pressure – but they also want to see how you respond to it as a guide to what your reaction would be under the pressures of the job you seek. They will be influenced by the degree of poise you display, the personal traits you show and the manner in which you respond.

EXAMINATION SECTION

ACCOUNTING
EXAMINATION SECTION
TEST 1

DIRECTIONS : Each question or incomplete statement is followed by several suggested answers or completions. Select the one that *BEST* answers the question or completes the statement. *PRINT THE LETTER OF THE CORRECT ANSWER IN THE SPACE AT THE RIGHT.*

Questions 1-5.

DIRECTIONS: Answer Questions 1 through 5 based on the information below.

When balance sheets are analyzed, working capital always receives close attention. Adequate working capital enables a company to carry sufficient inventories, meet current debts, take advantage of cash discounts and extend favorable terms to customers. A company that is deficient in working capital and unable to do these things is in a poor competitive position.

Below is a Trial Balance as of June 30, 2008, in alphabetical order, of the Worth Corporation:

	Debits	Credits
Accounts Payable		$ 50,000
Accounts Receivable	$ 40,000	
Accrued Expenses Payable		10,000
Capital Stock		10,000
Cash	20,000	
Depreciation Expense	5,000	
Inventory	60,000	
Plant & Equipment (net)	30,000	
Retained Earnings		20,000
Salary Expense	35,000	
Sales		100,000
	$190,000	$190,000

1. The Worth Corporation's Working Capital, based on the data above, is 1.____

   A. $50,000 B. $55,000 C. $60,000 D. $65,000

2. Which one of the following transactions increases Working Capital? 2.____

   A. Collecting outstanding accounts receivable
   B. Borrowing money from the bank based upon a 90-day interest-bearing note payable
   C. Paying off a 60-day note payable to the bank
   D. Selling merchandise at a profit

3. The Worth Corporation's Current Ratio, based on the above data, is 3.____

   A. 1.7 to 1 B. 2 to 1 C. 2.5 to 1 D. 4 to 3

4. Which one of the following transactions decreases the Current Ratio? 4.___

A. Collecting an account receivable
B. Borrowing money from the bank giving a 90-day interest-bearing note payable
C. Paying off a 60-day note payable to the bank
D. Selling merchandise at a profit

5. The payment of a current liability, such as Payroll Taxes Payable, will 5.___

A. *increase* the current ratio but have no effect on the working capital
B. *increase* the Working Capital, but have no effect on the current ratio
C. *decrease* both the current ratio and working capital
D. *increase* both the current ratio and working capital

6. During the year 2008, the Ramp Equipment Co. made sales to customers totaling $100,000 that were subject to sales taxes of $8,000. Net cash collections totaled $92,000. Discounts of $3,000 were allowed. During the year 2008, uncollectible accounts in the sum of $2,000 were written off the books. 6.___
The net change in accounts receivable during the year 2008 was

A. $10,500 B. $11,000 C. $13,000 D. $13,500

7. The Grable Co. received a $6,000, 8%, 60-day note dated May 1, 2008 from a customer. On May 16, 2008, the Grable Co. discounted the note at 6% at the bank. 7.___
The net proceeds from the discounting of the note amounted to

A. $5,954.40 B. $6,034.40 C. $6,064.80 D. $6,080.00

Question 8.

DIRECTIONS: Answer Question 8 based on the information below.

In reviewing the customers' accounts in the Accounts Receivable Ledger for the entire year 2007, the following errors are discovered

1. A sale in the amount of $500 to the J. Brown Co. was erroneously posted to the K. Brown Co.
2. A sales return of $100 from the Gale Co. was debited to their account
3. A check was received from a customer, M. White and Co. in payment of a sale of $500 less 2% discount. The check was entered properly in the cash receipts book but was posted to the M. White and Co. account in the amount of $490

8. The difference between the controlling account and its related accounts receivable schedule amounts to 8.___

A. $90 B. $110 C. $190 D. $210

9. Assume that you are called upon to audit a cash fund. You find in the cash drawer postage stamps and I.O.U.'s signed by employees, totaling together $425. 9.___
In preparing a financial report, the $425 should be reported as

A. petty cash B. investments
C. supplies and receivables D. cash

10. On December 31, 2008, before adjustment, Accounts Receivable had a debit balance of $60,000 and the Allowance for Uncollectible Accounts had a debit balance of $1,000. If credit losses are estimated at 5% of Accounts Receivable and the estimated method of reporting bad debts is used, then bad debts expense for the year 2008 would be reported as 10.____

A. $1,000 B. $2,000 C. $3,000 D. $4,000

Questions 11-12.

DIRECTIONS: Answer Questions 11 through 12 based on the information below.

Accrued salaries payable on $7,500 had not been recorded on December 31, 2008. Office supplies on hand of $2,500 at December 31, 2008 were erroneously treated as expense instead of inventory. Neither of these errors was discovered or corrected.

11. These two errors would cause the income for 2008 to be 11.____

A. *understated* by $5,000
B. *overstated* by $5,000
C. *understated* by $10,000
D. *overstated* by $10,000

12. The effect of these errors on the retained earnings at December 31, 2008 would be 12.____

A. *understated* by $2,500
B. *overstated* by $2,500
C. *understated* by $5,000
D. *overstated* by $5,000

Questions 13-14.

DIRECTIONS: Answer Questions 13 through 14 based on the information below.

Albano, Borrone, and Colluci operate a retail store under the trade name of ABC. Their partnership agreement provides for equally sharing profits and losses after salaries of $5,000 to Albano, $10,000 to Borrone, and $15,000 to Colluci.

13. If the net income of the partnership (prior to salaries to partners) is $21,000, then Albano's share of the profits, considering all aspects of the agreement, is determined to be 13.____

A. $2,000 B. $3,000 C. $5,000 D. $7,000

14. The share of the profits that apply to Borrone, similarly, is determined to be 14.____

A. $2,000 B. $3,000 C. $5,000 D. $7,000

Questions 15-17.

DIRECTIONS: Answer Questions 15 through 17 based on the information below.

The Kay Company currently uses FIFO for inventory valuation. Their records for the year ended June 30, 2008 reflect the following:

July 1, 2007 inventory	100,000 units @ $7.50
Purchases during year	400,000 units @ $8.00
Sales during year	350,000 units @ $15.00
Expenses exclusive of income taxes	$1,290,000
Cash Balance on June 30, 2007	$250,000
Income Tax Rate	45%

Assume the July 1, 2007 inventory will be the LIFO Base Inventory.

15. If the company should change to the LIFO as of June 30, 2008, then their income before taxes for the year-ended June 30, 2008, as compared with the income FIFO method, will be 15._

A. *increased* b $50,000
B. *decreased* by $50,000
C. *increased* by $100,000
D. *decreased* by $100,000

16. Assuming the given tax rate (45%), the use of the LIFO method will result in an approximate tax expense for fiscal 2008 of 16._

A. $45,000 B. $50,000 C. $72,000 D. $94,500

17. Assuming the given tax rate (45%), the use of the LIFO inventory method compared with the FIFO method, will result in a change in the approximate income tax expense for fiscal 2008 as follows: 17._

A. *Increase* of $22,500
B. *Decrease* of $22,500
C. *Increase* of $45,000
D. *Decrease* of $45,000

18. An accountant in an agency, in addition to his regular duties, has been assigned to train a newly appointed assistant accountant. The latter believes that he is not being given the training that he needs in order to perform his duties. 18._
Accordingly, the most appropriate FIRST step for the assistant accountant to take in order to secure the needed training is to

A. register for the appropriate courses at the local college as soon as possible
B. advise the accountant in a formal memo that his apparent lack of interest in the training is impeding his progress
C. discuss the matter with the accountant privately and try to discover what seems to be the problem
D. secure such training informally from more sympathetic accountants in the agency

19. You have worked very hard and successfully helped complete a difficult audit of a large corporation doing business with your agency. Your supervisor gives you a brief nod of approval when you expected a more substantial degree of recognition. You are angry and feel unappreciated. Of the following, the *most appropriate* course of action for you to take would be to 19._

A. voice your displeasure to your fellow workers at being taken for granted by an unappreciative supervisor
B. say nothing now and assume that your supervisor's nod of approval may be his customary acknowledgment of efforts well done
C. let your supervisor know that he owes you something by repeatedly stressing the outstanding job you've done
D. ease off on your work quality and productivity until your efforts are finally appreciated

20. You have been assisting in an audit of the books and records of businesses as a member of a team. The accountant in charge of your group tells you to start preliminary work independently on a new audit. This audit is to take place at the offices of the business. The business officers have been duly notified of the audit date. Upon arrival at their offices, you find that their records and files are in disarray and that their personnel are antagonistic and uncooperative. Of the following, the *most desirable* action for you to take is to 20.____

A. advise the business officers that serious consequences may follow unless immediate cooperation is secured
B. accept whatever may be shown or told you on the grounds that it would be unwise to further antagonize uncooperative personnel
C. inform your supervisor of the situation and request instructions
D. leave immediately and return later in the expectation of encountering a more cooperative attitude.

KEY (CORRECT ANSWERS)

1.	C	11.	C
2.	D	12.	A
3.	B	13.	A
4.	B	14.	D
5.	A	15.	B
6.	B	16.	C
7.	B	17.	B
8.	D	18.	C
9.	C	19.	B
10.	D	20.	C

TEST 2

DIRECTIONS : Each question or incomplete statement is followed by several suggested answers or completions. Select the one that *BEST* answers the question or completes the statement. *PRINT THE LETTER OF THE CORRECT ANSWER IN THE SPACE AT THE RIGHT.*

Questions 1-3.

DIRECTIONS: Answer Questions 1 through 3 based on the following.

The city is planning to borrow money with a 5-year, 7% bond issue totaling $10,000,000 on principal when other municipal issues are paying 8%.

Present value of $ 1 - 8% - 5 years - .68058
Present value of annual interest payments - annuity 8% - 5 years -3.99271

1. The funds obtained from this bond issue (ignoring any costs related to issuance) would be, approximately, 1.___

   A. $9,515,390
   B. $10,000,000
   C. $10,484,610
   D. $10,800,000

2. At the date of maturity, the bonds will be redeemed at 2.___

   A. $9,515,390
   B. $10,000,000
   C. $10,484,610
   D. $10,800,000

3. As a result of this issue, the *actual* interest costs each year as related to the 7% interest payments will 3.___

   A. be the same as paid ($700,000)
   B. be more than $700,000
   C. be less than $700,000
   D. fluctuate depending on the market conditions

4. Following the usual governmental accounting concepts, the activities of a municipal employee retirement plan, which is financed by equal employer and employee contributions, should be accounted for in a(n) 4.___

   A. agency fund
   B. intragovernmental service fund
   C. special assessment fund
   D. trust fund

Questions 5-7.

DIRECTIONS: Answer Questions 5 through 7 based on the following.

The Balance Sheet of the JLA Corp. is as follows:

Current assets	$50,000	Current liabilities	$20,000
Other assets	75,000	Common stock	75,000
Total	$125,000	Retained earnings	30,000
		Total	$125,000

5. The working capital of the JLA Corp. is 5.____

A. $30,000 B. $50,000 C. $105,000 D. $125,000

6. The operating ratio of the JLA Corp. is 6.____

A. 2 to 1 B. $2\frac{1}{2}$ to 1 C. 1 to 2 D. 1 to $2\frac{1}{2}$

7. The stockholders' equity is 7.____

A. $30,000 B. $75,000 C. $105,000 D. $125,000

Question 8.

DIRECTIONS: Answer Question 8 based on the following figures taken from a set of books for the year ending June 30, 2008.

	Trial Balance Before Adjustments	Trial Balance After Adjustments
Commissions Payable	cr ---	cr $ 1,550
Office Salaries	dr $9,500	dr $10,680
Rental Income	cr $4,300	cr $ 4,900
Accumulated Depreciation	cr $7,000	cr $ 9,700
Supplies Expense	dr $1,760	dr $ 1,200

8. As a result of the adjustments reflected in the adjusted trial balance, the net income of the company before taxes will be 8.____

A. *increased* by $4,270
B. *decreased* by $4,270
C. *increased* by $5,430
D. *decreased* by $5,430

Question 9.

DIRECTIONS: Answer Question 9 based on the following facts concerning the operations of a manufacturer of office desks.

Jan. 1, 2008	Goods in Process Inventory	4,260 units	40% complete
Dec. 31, 2008	Goods in Process Inventory	3,776 units	25% complete
Jan. 1, 2008	Finished Goods Inventory	2,630 units	
Dec. 31, 2008	Finished Goods Inventory	3,180 units	

Sales consummated during the year-127,460 units

9. Assuming that all the desks are the same style, the number of equivalent complete units, manufactured during the year 2008 is: 9.____

A. 127,250 B. 127,460 C. 128,010 D. 131,510

Questions 10-11.

DIRECTIONS: Answer Questions 10 through 11 based on the following.

On January 1, 2008, the Lenox Corporation was organized with a cash investment of $50,000 by the shareholders. Some of the corporate records were destroyed. However you were able to discover the following facts from various sources:

Accounts Payable at December 31, 2008 (arising from merchandise purchased)	$16,000
Accounts Receivable at December 31, 2008 (arising from the sales of merchandise)	18,000
Sales for the calendar year 2008	94,000
Inventory, December 31, 2008	20,000
Cost of Goods Sold is 60% of the selling price	
Bank loan outstanding - December 31, 2008	15,000
Expenses paid in cash during the year	35,000
Expenses incurred but unpaid as of December 31, 2008	4,000
Dividend paid	25,000

10. The *correct* cash balance is 10.___

A. $5,600 B. $20,600 C. $38,600 D. $40,600

11. The stockholders' equity on December 31, 2008 is 11.___

A. $23,600
B. Deficit of $26,400
C. $27,600
D. $42,400

Questions 12-13.

DIRECTIONS: Answer Questions 12 and 13 based on the following facts developed from the records of a company that sells its merchandise on the installment plan.

Sales	Calendar Year 2007	Calendar Year 2008
Total volume of sales	$80,000	$100,000
Cost of Goods Sold	60,000	40,000
Gross Profit	$20,000	$ 60,000
Cash Collections		
From 2007 Sales	$18,000	$36,000
From 2008 Sales		22,000
Total Cash Collections	$18,000	$58,000

12. Using the deferred profit method of determining the income from installment sales, the gross profit on sales for the calendar year 2007 was 12.___

A. $4,500 B. $18,000 C. $20,000 D. None

13. Using the deferred profit method of determining the income from installment sales, the gross profit on sales for the calendar year 2008 was 13.___

A. $22,000 B. $22,200 C. $60,000 D. None

Questions 14-15.

DIRECTIONS: Answer Questions 14 through 15 based on the following data developed from an examination of the records of Ralston, Inc. for the month of April 2008.

Beginning inventory: 10,000 units @ $4.00 each

Purchases			Sales		
April 10	20,000	units @ $5 each	April 13	15,000 units	@ $8 each
17	60,000	units @ $6 each	21	50,000 units	@ $9 each
26	40,000	units @ $7 each	27	50,000 units	@ $10 each

14. The gross profit on sales for the month of April, 2008, assuming that inventory is priced on the FIFO basis, is 14.____

A. $330,000 B. $355,000 C. $395,000 D. $435,000

15. The gross profit on sales for the month of April, 2008, assuming that inventory is priced on the LIFO basis, is 15.____

A. $330,000 B. $355,000 C. $395,000 D. $435,000

Question 16.

DIRECTIONS: Answer Question 16 based on the data presented for June 30, 2008.

Balance per Bank Statement	$24,019.00
Balance per General Ledger	20,592.64
Proceeds of note collected by the bank which had not been recorded in the Cash account	4,000.00
Interest on note collected by the bank (no book entries made)	39.40
Debit memo for Bank charges for the month of May	23.50
Deposit in Transit (June 30, 2008)	2,144.00
Customer's check returned by the bank due to lack of funds	150.00
Outstanding checks - June 30, 2008	1,631.46
Error in recording check made by our bookkeeper - check cleared in the amount of $463.00 but entered in the bank book for $436.00	

16. If we wish to reconcile the bank and book balance so that the bank balance and the book balance are reconciled to a corrected balance, the corrected balance should be 16.____

A. $20,592.64 B. $24,019.00 C. $24,531.54 D. $26,163.00

17. The Ateb Company has issued a $500,000 bond issue on January 1, 2007, at 8% interest, payable semi-annually, sold at par, with interest payable on June 30 and December 31. 17.____
On September 30, 2007, at the close of the fiscal year of the Ateb Company, the interest expense accrual should reflect interest payable of, approximately,

A. $10,000 B. $20,000 C. $40,000 D. $50,000

18. Assume that a new procedure requires that a particular and unvarying sequence of steps be followed in order to yield the desired data. You are assigned to be in charge of subordinates working with this procedure. 18.____
Which one of the following is *most likely* to impress subordinates with the importance of following the sequence of steps exactly as given?

A. *Explain* the consequences of error if the procedure is not followed
B. *Suggest* how rewarding would be the feeling of finding errors before the supervisor catches them
C. *Indicate* that independent verification of their work will be done by other staff members
D. *Advise* that upward career mobility usually results from following instructions exactly

19. It is essential for an experienced accountant to know approximately how long it will take him to complete a particular assignment because 19.__

A. his supervisors will need to obtain this information only from someone planning to perform the assignment
B. he must arrange his schedule to insure proper completion of the assignment consistent with agency objectives
C. he must measure whether he is keeping pace with others performing similar assignments
D. he must determine what assignments are essential and have the greatest priority within his agency

20. There are circumstances which call for special and emergency efforts by employees. You must assign your staff to make this type of effort. 20.__
Of the following, this special type of assignment is *most likely* to succeed if the

A. time schedule required to complete the assignment is precisely stated but is not adhered to
B. employees are individually free to determine the work schedule
C. assignment is clearly defined
D. employees are individually free to use any procedure or method available to them

---

KEY (CORRECT ANSWERS)

1.	A	11.	A
2.	B	12.	A
3.	B	13.	B
4.	D	14.	C
5.	A	15.	B
6.	B	16.	C
7.	C	17.	A
8.	B	18.	A
9.	A	19.	B
10.	B	20.	C

EXAMINATION SECTION
TEST 1

DIRECTIONS: Each question or incomplete statement is followed by several suggested answers or completions. Select the one that BEST answers the question or completes the statement. *PRINT THE LETTER OF THE CORRECT ANSWER IN THE SPACE AT THE RIGHT.*

1. The independent auditor's PRIMARY objective in reviewing internal control is to provide 1.____

   A. assurance of the client's operational efficiency
   B. a basis for reliance on the system and determination of the scope of the auditing procedures
   C. a basis for suggestions for improving the client's accounting system
   D. evidence of the client's adherence to prescribed managerial policies

2. If there is an increase in work-in-process inventory during a period, 2.____

   A. cost of goods sold will be greater than cost of goods manufactured
   B. cost of goods manufactured will be greater than cost of goods sold
   C. manufacturing costs (production costs) for the period will be greater than cost of goods manufactured
   D. manufacturing costs for the period will be less than cost of goods manufactured

Questions 3-4.

DIRECTIONS: Answer questions 3 and 4 on the basis of the information given below about the Parr Company and the Farr Company.

The Parr Company purchased 800 of the 1,000 outstanding shares of the Farr Company's common stock for $80,000 on January 1, 2004. During 2004, the Farr Company declared dividends of $8,000 and reported earnings for the year of $20,000.

3. Using the equity method, the investment in Farr Company on the Parr Company's books should show a balance, at December 31, 2004, of 3.____

   A. $89,600 B. $86,400 C. $80,000 D. $73,600

4. If, instead of using the equity method, the Parr Company uses the cost method, the balance, at December 31, 2004, in the investment account, should be 4.____

   A. $96,000 B. $86,400 C. $80,000 D. $73,600

Questions 5-6.

DIRECTIONS: Answer questions 5 and 6 on the basis of the information given below about the Fame Corporation.

The Fame Corporation has 50,000 shares of $10 par value common stock authorized, issued and outstanding. The 50,000 shares were issued at $12 per share. The retained earnings of the company are $60,000.

5. Assuming that the Fame Corporation reacquired 1,000 of its common shares at $15 per share and the par value method of accounting for treasury stock was used, the result would be that 5.__

A. stockholders' equity would increase by $15,000
B. capital in excess of par would decrease by at least $2,000
C. retained earnings would decrease by $5,000
D. common stock would decrease by at least $15,000

6. Assuming that the Fame Corporation reissued 1,000 of its common shares at $11 per share and the cost method of accounting for treasury stock was used, the result would be that 6.__

A. book value per share of common stock would decrease
B. retained earnings would decrease by $11,000
C. donated surplus would be credited for $5,500
D. a gain on reissue of treasury stock account would be charged

7. On January 31, 2004, when the Montana Corporation's stock was selling at $36 per share, its capital accounts were as follows: 7.__

Capital Stock (par value $20; 100,000 shares issued)	$2,000,000
Premium on Capital Stock	800,000
Retained Earnings	4,550,000

If the corporation declares a 100% stock dividend and the par value per share remains at $20, the value of the capital stock would

A. remain the same
B. increase to $5,600,000
C. increase to $5,000,000
D. decrease

8. In a conventional form of the statement of sources and application of funds, which one of the following would NOT be included? 8.__

A. Periodic amortization of premium of bonds payable
B. Machinery, fully depreciated and scrapped
C. Patents written off
D. Treasury stock purchased from a stockholder

Questions 9-11.

DIRECTIONS: Answer questions 9 through 11 on the basis of the balance sheet shown below for the Argo, Baron and Schooster partnership.

Cash	$ 20,000
Other assets	180,000
Total	$200,000
Liabilities	$ 50,000
Argo Capital (40%)	37,000
Baron Capital (40%)	65,000
Schooster Capital (20%)	48,000
Total	$200,000

9. If George is to be admitted as a new 1/6 partner without recording goodwill or bonus, George should contribute cash of 9.____

A. $40,000 B. $36,000 C. $33,333 D. $30,000

10. Assume that Schooster is paid $51,000 by George for his interest in the partnership. Which of the following choices shows the CORRECT revised capital account for each partner? 10.____

A. Argo $38,500; Baron $66,500; George $51,000
B. Argo $38,500; Baron $66,500; George $48,000
C. Argo $37,000; Baron $65,000; George $51,000
D. Argo $37,000; Baron $65,000; George $48,000

11. Assume that George had not been admitted as a partner but that the partnership was dissolved and liquidated on the basis of the original balance sheet. Non-cash assets with a book value of $90,000 were sold for $50,000 cash. After payment of creditors, all available cash was distributed. 11.____
Which of the following choices MOST NEARLY shows what each of the partners would receive?

A. Argo $0; Baron $13,333; Schooster $6,667
B. Argo $0; Baron $3,000; Schooster $17,000
C. Argo $6,667; Baron $6,667; Schooster $6,666
D. Argo $8,000; Baron $8,000; Schooster $4,000

12. Which one of the following should be restricted to ONLY one employee in order to assure proper control of assets? 12.____

A. Access to safe deposit box
B. Placing orders and maintaining relationship with a principal vendor
C. Collection of a particular past due account
D. Custody of the petty cash fund

13. To assure proper internal control, the quantities of materials ordered may be omitted from that copy of the purchase order which is 13.____

A. sent to the accounting department
B. retained in the purchasing department
C. sent to the party requisitioning the material
D. sent to the receiving department

14. The Amey Corporation has an inventory of raw materials and parts made up of many different items which are of small value individually but of significant total value. A BASIC control requirement in such a situation is that 14.____

A. perpetual inventory records should be maintained for all items
B. physical inventories should be taken on a cyclical basis rather than at year end
C. storekeeping, production and inventory record-keeping functions should be separated
D. requisitions for materials should be approved by a corporate officer

15. In conducting an audit of plant assets, which of the following accounts MUST be examined in order to ascertain that additions to plant assets have been correctly stated and reflect charges that are properly capitalized? 15._

A. Accounts Receivable
B. Sales Income
C. Maintenance and Repairs
D. Investments

16. Which one of the following is a control procedure that would prevent a vendor's invoice from being paid *twice* (once upon the original invoice and once upon the monthly statement)? 16._

A. Attaching the receiving report to the disbursement support papers
B. Prenumbering of disbursement vouchers
C. Using a limit or reasonable test
D. Prenumbering of receiving reports

17. A "cut-off" bank statement is received for the period December 1 to December 10, 2004. Very few of the checks listed on the November 30, 2004 bank reconciliation cleared during the cut-off period. Of the following, the MOST likely reason for this is 17._

A. kiting
B. using certified checks rather than ordinary checks
C. holding the cash disbursement book open after year end
D. overstating year-end bank balance

18. "Lapping" is a common type of defalcation. Of the audit techniques listed below, the one MOST effective in the detection of "lapping" is 18._

A. reconciliation of year-end bank statements
B. review of duplicate deposit slips
C. securing confirmations from banks
D. checking footings in cash journals

19. Of the following, the MOST common argument against the use of the negative accounts receivable confirmation is that 19._

A. cost per response is excessively high
B. statistical sampling techniques cannot be applied to selection of the sample
C. client's customers may assume that the confirmation is a request for payment
D. lack of response does not necessarily indicate agreement with the balance

Questions 20-21.

DIRECTIONS: Answer questions 20 and 21 on the basis of the information in the Payroll Summary given below. This Payroll Summary represents payroll for a monthly period for a particular agency.

PAYROLL SUMMARY

Employee	Total Earnings	FICA	Withhold. Tax	State Tax	Other	Net Pay
		Deductions				
W	450.00	26.00	67.00	18.00	6.00	333.00
X	235.00	14.00	33.00	8.00	2.00	178.00
Y	341.00	20.00	52.00	14.00	5.00	250.00
Z	275.00	16.00	30.00	6.00	2.40	220.60
Totals	1,301.00	76.00	182.00	46.00	15.40	981.60

20. Based on the data given above, the amount of cash that would have to be available to pay the employees on payday is 20.____

A. $1301.00 B. $981.60 C. $905.60 D. $662.60

21. Based on the data given above, the amount required to be deposited with a governmental depository is 21.____

A. $334.00 B. $182.00 C. $158.00 D. $76.00

Questions 22-23.

DIRECTIONS: Answer questions 22 and 23 based on the information given below concerning an imprest fund.

Assume a $1,020 imprest fund for cash expenditures is maintained in your agency. As an audit procedure, the fund is counted and the following information results from that count:

Unreimbursed bills properly authorized	$345.00
Check from employee T. Jones	125.00
Check from Supervisor R. Riggles	250.00
I.O.U. signed by employee J. Sloan	100.00
Cash counted - coins and bills	200.00
TOTAL	$1,020.00

22. A PROPER statement of cash on hand based upon the data shown above should show a balance of 22.____

A. $1,020 B. $1,000 C. $545 D. $200

23. Based upon the data shown above, the account reflects IMPROPER handling of the fund because 23.____

A. vouchers are unreimbursed
B. the cash balance is too low
C. employees have used it for loans and check-cashing purposes
D. the unreimbursed bills should not have been authorized

Questions 24-25.

DIRECTIONS: Answer questions 24 and 25 based on the information below.

The following information was taken from the ledgers of the Past Present Corporation:

Common stock had been issued for $6,000,000. This represented 400,000 shares of stock at a stated value of $5 per share. Fifty-thousand shares are in the treasury. These 50,000 shares were acquired for $25 per share. The total undistributed net income since the origin of the corporation was $3,750,000 as of December 31, 2004. Ten-thousand of the treasury stock shares were sold in January 2005 for $30 per share.

24. Based only on the information given above, the TOTAL stockholders' equity that should have been shown on the balance sheet as of December 31, 2004 was 24.___

A. $2,000,000
B. $6,000,000
C. $8,500,000
D. $9,750,000

25. Based only on the information given above, the Retained Earnings as of December 31, 2005, will be 25.___

A. $2,000,000
B. $3,750,000
C. $3,800,000
D. $4,050,000

Questions 26-29.

DIRECTIONS: Answer questions 26 through 29 on the basis of the information given below.

A statement of income for the Dartmouth Corporation for the 2004 fiscal year follows:

Sales	$89,000	
Cost of Goods Sold	20,000	
Gross Margin		$34,000
Expenses		20.000
Net Income before IncomeTaxes		$14,000
Provision for Income Taxes (50%)		7.000
Net Income		$ 7,000

The following errors were discovered relating to the 2004 fiscal year:

- Closing inventory was overstated by $2,100.
- A $3,000 expenditure was capitalized during fiscal year 2004 that should have been listed under Expenses.This was subject to 10% amortization taken for a full year.
- Sales included $3,500 of deposits received from customers for future orders.
- Accrued salaries of $850 were not included in Cost of Goods Sold.
- Interest receivable of $500 was omitted.

Assume that the books were not closed and that you have prepared a corrected income statement. Answer questions 26 through 29 on the basis of your corrected income statement.

26. The gross margin after accounting for adjustments SHOULD BE 26.___

A. $37,500 B. $35,400 C. $31,900 D. $27,550

27. The adjusted income before income taxes SHOULD BE 27.___

A. $5,350 B. $9,550 C. $15,000 D. $15,850

28. The adjusted income after provision for a 50% tax rate SHOULD BE 28.___

A. $7,925 B. $7,500 C. $4,500 D. $2,675

29. After making adjustments, sales to be reported for fiscal year 2004 SHOULD BE 29.___

A. unchanged
B. increased by $3,500
C. decreased by $3,500
D. reduced by $2,100

Questions 30-33.

DIRECTIONS: Answer questions 30 through 33 based on the following budget for the Utility Corporation for 2004:

Sales	$550,000
Cost of goods sold	320,000
Selling expenses	75,000
General expenses	60,000
Net income	95,000

30. If sales are actually 12% above the budget, then ACTUAL sales will be 30.____

A. $550,000 B. $562,000 C. $605,000 D. $616,000

31. If actual costs of goods sold exceed the budget by 10%, then the cost of goods sold will be 31.____

A. $294,400 B. $320,000 C. $345,600 D. $352,000

32. If selling expenses exceed the budget by 10%, the INCREASE in the selling expenses will be 32.____

A. $750 B. $3,750 C. $7,500 D. $8,333

33. If general expenses are under budget by 5%, they will amount to 33.____

A. $3,000 B. $57,000 C. $60,000 D. $63,000

Questions 34-35.

DIRECTIONS: Answer questions 34 and 35 on the basis of the following information.

The Yontiff Company began business on January 2, 2004. During the first month, credit sales totaled $100,000. During February, credit sales totaled $125,000. 70% of credit sales are paid during the month of sale, and the balance is collected during the following month.

34. During the month of January, cash collections on credit sales totaled 34.____

A. $70,000 B. $95,000 C. $100,000 D. $125,000

35. During the month of February, cash collections on credit sales totaled 35.____

A. $70,000 B. $87,500 C. $117,500 D. $125,000

Questions 36-38.

DIRECTIONS: Answer questions 36 through 38 on the basis of the following information taken from the balance sheet of the F Corporation.

Common Stock $200 par	$1 ,400,000
Premium on Common Stock	115,000
Deficit	50,000

36. The number of shares of common stock outstanding is 36.____

A. 200 B. 700 C. 7,000 D. 14,000

37. The total equity is 37.___

A. $50,000
B. $115,000
C. $1,400,000
D. $1,465,000

38. The book value per share of stock is, MOST NEARLY, 38.___

A. $160
B. $200
C. $209
D. $312

Questions 39-40.

DIRECTIONS: Answer questions 39 and 40 based on the following statement.

You are examining the expense accounts of a contractor and you discover that, although his payroll records show proper deductions from employees, he has never provided for the payroll tax expenses for these employees.

39. As a result of the oversight described in the above statement, the Costs of Construction in Progress as given on the balance sheet will be 39.___

A. understated on the balance sheet
B. overstated on the balance sheet
C. unaffected on the balance sheet
D. omitted from the balance sheet

40. As a result of the oversight described in the above statement, the balance sheet for the firm will reflect on 40.___

A. overstatement of liabilities
B. understatement of liabilities
C. overstatement of assets
D. understatement of assets

KEY (CORRECT ANSWERS)

1.	B	11.	D	21.	A	31.	D
2.	C	12.	D	22.	D	32.	C
3.	A	13.	D	23.	C	33.	B
4.	C	14.	C	24.	C	34.	A
5.	B	15.	C	25.	B	35.	C
6.	A	16.	A	26.	D	36.	C
7.	A	17.	C	27.	A	37.	D
8.	B	18.	B	28.	D	38.	C
9.	D	19.	D	29.	C	39.	A
10.	D	20.	B	30.	D	40.	B

TEST 2

DIRECTIONS: Each question or incomplete statement is followed by several suggested answers or completions. Select the one that BEST answers the question or completes the statement. *PRINT THE LETTER OF THE CORRECT ANSWER IN THE SPACE AT THE RIGHT.*

Questions 1-4.

In the audit of the Audell Co. for the calendar year 2004, the accountant noted the following errors:

- An adjusting entry for $10 for interest accrued on a customer's $4,000, 60-day, 6% note was not recorded at the end of December 2003. In 2004 the total interest received was credited to Interest Income.
- Equipment was leased on December 1, 2003, and rental of $300 was paid in advance for the next three months and charged to Rent Expense.
- On November 1, 2003, space was rented at $75 per month. The tenant paid six months rent in advance which was credited to Rent Income.
- Salary expenses in the amount of $60 were not recorded at the end of 2003.
- Depreciation in the amount of $80 was not recorded at the end of 2003.
- An error of $200 in addition on the year-end 2003 physical inventory sheets was made. The inventory was overstated.

1. The amount of the net adjustment to Net Income for 2003 is 1.____

   A. Credit $430 B. Debit $430
   C. Credit $600 D. Credit $560

2. The net change in asset values at December 31, 2003 is 2.____

   A. Credit $70 B. Debit $70
   C. Debit $110 D. Credit $60

3. The net change in liabilities at December 31, 2003 is 3.____

   A. Debit $360 B. Credit $430
   C. Debit $560 D. Credit $360

4. The net change in Owner's Equity at December 31, 2003 is 4.____

   A. Debit $710 B. Debit $430
   C. Credit $320 D. Credit $710

5. As of October 31, 2004, the Mallory Company's books reflect a balance of $2,104.75 in its account entitled, Cash in Bank. A comparison of the book entries with the bank statement showed the following: 5.____

   - A check in the amount of $76.25 outstanding at the end of September 2004 had not been returned.
   - One check, which was returned with the October bank statement, in the amount of $247 had been recorded in the October cash book as $274.
   - A total of $139 of checks issued in October had not been returned with the October bank statement.
   - A deposit of $65 was returned by the bank because of insufficient funds.

- The bank charged a service charge of $3.25 for the month of October which was not reported on the books until November.
- The bank had credited $247 representing a note collected in the amount of $250 which was not picked up on the books until November.
- A deposit of $305.50 was recorded on the books in October but not on the bank statement.

The balance in the bank as shown on the bank statement at October 31, 2004 is
A. $2,220.25 B. $2,104.75 C. $2,006.25 D. $2,315.25

Questions 6-8.

A company purchased three cars at $3,150 each on April 2, 2003. Depreciation is to be computed on a mileage basis. The estimated mileage to be considered is 50,000 miles, with a trade-in value of $650 for each car.

After having been driven 8,400 miles, car #1 was completely destroyed on November 23, 2003 and not replaced. The insurance company paid $2,500 for the loss.

As of December 31, 2003, of the two remaining cars, car #2 had been driven 10,300 miles and car #3 was driven 11,500 miles.

On July 10, 2004, after having been driven a total of 24,600 miles, car #2 was sold for $1,800.

Car #3, after having been driven a total of 27,800 miles, was traded in on December 28, 2004 for a new car (#4) that had a list price of $3,000. On the purchase of car #4, the dealer allowed a trade-in value of $1,850.

6. The balance in the Allowance for Depreciation account at December 31, 2003 is 6

A. $1,850 B. $910 C. $1,090 D. $1,110

7. The depreciation expense for the calendar year 2004 is 7

A. $1,530 B. $2,000 C. $2,500 D. $3,000

8. The book value of the new car (car #4), using the income tax method, is 8

A. $1,850 B. $3,000 C. $2,500 D. $2,910

Questions 9-10.

The Pneumatic Corp. showed the following balance sheets at December 31, 2003 and December 31, 2004:

	12/31/2003	12/31/2004
Cash	$6,700	$9,000
Accounts Receivable	12,000	11,500
Merchandise Inventory	31,500	32,000
Prepaid Expenses	800	1,000
Equipment	21,000	28,000
	$72,000	$81,500
Accumulated Depreciation	$4,000	$5,500
Accounts Payable	17,500	11,000
Common Stock- $5 per share	10,000	5,000
Premium on Common Stock	40,000	50,000
Retained Earnings	10,500	13,000
	$72,000	$81,500

Additional information - A further examination of the Pneumatic Corp.'s transactions for 2004 showed the following:

- Depreciation on equipment $2,500
- Fully depreciated equipment that cost $1,000 was scrapped, and cost and related accumulated depreciation eliminated.
- Two thousand shares of common stock were sold at $6 per share.
- A cash dividend of $10,000 was paid.

9. A statement of funds provided and applied for the calendar year 2004 would show that net income provided funds in the amount of 9.____

   A. $2,500 B. $9,500 C. $15,000 D. $22,500

10. The funds applied to the acquisition of equipment during the calendar year 2004 amounts to 10.____

   A. $21,000 B. $28,000 C. $1,000 D. $8,000

11. A company's Wage Expense account had a $19,100 debit balance before any adjustment at the end of its December 31, 2004 fiscal year. The company employs five individuals who earn $15 per day and were paid on Friday for the five days ending on Friday, December 26, 2004. All employees worked during the week ending January 2, 2005. The adjusted balance in the Wage Expense account at December 31, 2004 is 11.____

   A. $22,300 B. $19,100 C. $19,250 D. $19,325

Questions 12-13.

The Peach Corp.'s books reflect an account entitled "Allowance for Bad Debts" showing a credit balance of $1,510 as of January 1, 2003.

During 2003, it wrote off $735 of bad debts and increased the allowance for bad debts by an amount equal to 1/4 of 1% of sales of $408,000.

During 2004, it wrote off $605 as bad debts and recorded $50 of a debt that had been previously written off.

An addition to the "Allowance for Bad Debts" was provided based upon 1/4 of 1% on $478,000 of sales.

12. The balance in the "Allowance for Bad Debts" account at December 31, 2004 is 12.____

   A. $2,550 B. $2,435 C. $2,360 D. $2,240

13. The amount of the Bad Debt expense for the calendar year 2004 is 13.____

   A. $1,195 B. $1,405 C. $1,000 D. $1,510

14. The following ratio is based upon the 2004 financial statements of the Chino Corp.: 14.____

   Number of Times Bond Interest Earned:

   $28,000 / $3,000 = 9.33 times

   Information relating to the corrections of the income data for 2004 follows:

   - Rental payment for December 2004 at $1,200 per month had been recorded in January 2005. No provision had been made for this expense on the 2004 books.

- During 2004, merchandise shipped on consignment and unsold had been recorded as

Debit - Accounts Receivable	$4,000
Credit - Sales	4,000

(Note: The inventory of this merchandise was properly recorded.)

If the described ratio, Number of Times Bond Interest Earned, was recomputed, taking into consideration the corrections listed above and ignoring income tax factors in the calculations, the recomputed Number of Times Bond Interest Earned would be

A. 8.10 times B. 7.60 times
C. 6.20 times D. 5.10 times

Questions 15-16.

The Delancey Department Store, Inc. sells merchandise on the installment basis. The selling price of its merchandise is $500 and its cost is $325.

At the end of its fiscal year an examination of its accounts showed the following:

Sales (Installment)	$500,000
Installment Accounts Receivable	280,000
Sales Commissions	15,000
Other Expenses	32,000

15. The net income for the fiscal year, before taxes, using the installment method of reporting income, is 15._

A. $30,000 B. $20,000 C. $15,000 D. $35,000

16. The balance in the Deferred Income Account at the end of the fiscal year is 16._

A. $110,000 B. $80,000 C. $76,000 D. $98,000

Questions 17-18.

The Merrimac Company sold 8,800 units of a product at $5 per unit during the calendar year 2004. In addition, it had the following transactions:

	Units	Unit Cost
Inventory - January 1, 2004	1,000	$2.80
Purchases - March	1,000	3.00
June	4,000	3.20
September	3,000	3.30
October	1,000	3.50

17. If we assume that selling and administrative expenses cost $8,800, the Net Income for the calendar year 2004, using the first-in first-out method of costing inventory, is 17._

A. $8,460 B. $7,360 C. $6,600 D. $4,070

18. If we assume that selling and administrative expenses cost $8,800, the Net Income for the calendar year 2004, using the last-in first-out method of costing inventory, is 18._

A. $4,550 B. $7,360 C. $6,600 D. $5,000

19. L. Eron and A. Pilott are partners who share income and losses in the ratio of 3:2, respectively. The balance in the Profit and Loss account on December 31, 2004, prior to distribution to the partners, is $20,800. Before distributing any profits to the partnership in the agreed ratio, L. Eron is to be given credit for interest on his loan of $60,000, outstanding for the entire year, at 6% per annum. A. Pilott is to receive a bonus of 10% of the net income over $5,100, after deducting the bonus to himself and the interest to L. Eron. Giving consideration to all the above information, the total amount of net income to be credited to A. Pilott is 19.____

A. $8,320 B. $2,080 C. $7,540 D. $15,700

Questions 20-21.

Schneider and Samuels are partners with capital balances on December 31, 2004 of $15,000 and $25,000, respectively. They share profits in a ratio of 2:1.

Goroff is to be admitted to the partnership. He agrees to be admitted as a partner with a cash investment to give him a one-third interest in the capital and profits of the business. All the parties agree that the good will to be granted to Goroff should be valued at $6,000.

20. The required cash to cover Goroff's investment in a business partnership according to the terms stated is 20.____

A. $20,000 B. $14,000 C. $6,000 D. $25,000

21. After his cash investment, and all other initial entries, the credit to Goroff's Capital account is 21.____

A. $20,000 B. $14,000 C. $6,000 D. $25,000

22. The Marlin Corp. sold 7,800 units of its product at $25 per unit and suffered a net loss for its calendar year ending December 31, 2003 of $2,000. 22.____
The fixed expenses amounted to $80,000 and the variable expenses $117,000. The Marlin Corp. believes that by expending $20,000 in an advertising campaign, it could increase its sales, retaining the $25 per unit selling price, to generate a profit.
Assuming the above facts, the sales revenue for 2003 reflecting the break-even point is

A. $195,000 B. $217,000 C. $250,000 D. $300,000

23. The Anide Corp., which keeps its books on the accrual basis, had the following transactions for its calendar year ending December 31, 2004: 23.____
- April 15, 2004 - Authorized the issuance of $3,000,000 of 5.5%, 20 year bonds, dated May 1, 2004. Interest to be paid November 1 and May 1.
- June 1, 2004 - Sold the entire issue at $2,964,150 plus accrued interest.
- November 1, 2004 - Paid the interest due.

The interest expense for the calendar year ending December 31, 2004 is

A. $85,000 B. $165,000 C. $110,000 D. $97,300

Questions 24-26.

The following information was taken from a worksheet that was used in the preparation of the balance sheet and the profit and loss statement of the Hott Company for 2004:

The Balance Sheet Contained	Amount
Travel Expense Unpaid	$995
Legal and Collection Fees - Prepaid in Advance	672
Interest Received in Advance	469

The Profit and Loss Statement Contained	Amount
Travel Expenses	$7,343
Legal and Collection Fees	5,461
Interest Income	3,114

The proper adjusting and closing entries were made on the books of the company by the accountant and the described information was reported on the financial statements. The books are kept on an accrual basis.

On the basis of the above facts, the balance in each of the following accounts in the trial balance, *before adjusting and closing entries were made,* was as follows:

24. Travel Expense Account 24._

A. $8,338 B. $7,343 C. $6,348 D. $995

25. Legal and Collection Fees Account 25._

A. $672 B. $4,789 C. $5,461 D. $6,133

26. Interest Income Account 26._

A. $3,583 B. $3,114 C. $2,645 D. $469

Questions 27-28.

The following is the stockholder's equity section of a corporation:

Preferred Stock (7%, cumulative, non-participating, $100 par value, 5,000 shares issued and outstanding)	$ 500,000
Common Stock ($1.00 par value, 500,000 issued and outstanding)	500,000
	1,000,000
Deficit	(40,000)
	$ 960,000

27. Assuming two years' dividends in arrears on the preferred stock, the book value per share of common stock is 27._

A. 78¢ B. 80¢ C. 63¢ D. 94¢

28. Assuming two years' dividends in arrears on the preferred stock, the book value per share of preferred stock is 28.____

A. $130   B. $114   C. $98   D. $140

Questions 29-30.

Regina Corporation on December 31, 2003 had the following stockholder's equity:

Common Stock ($10 par value, 10,000 shares authorized and outstanding)	$100,000
Retained Earnings	20,000
	$120,000

On December 31, 2003, the Astro Corp. purchased 9,000 shares of the Regina Corporation's outstanding shares, paying $14 per share.

29. The entry to eliminate Astro Corp.'s investment and the Regina Corporation's stockholder's equity on consolidation would show a debit or credit to an account called "Excess of Cost Over Book Value" of 29.____

A. Credit $18,000
B. Debit $18,000
C. Debit $15,000
D. Debit $19,000

30. If the Regina Corporation had earnings for the calendar year 2004 of $10,000 and had paid out $8,000 of these earnings as dividends, and an entry to eliminate the Astro Corp.'s investment and the Regina Corporation's stockholder's equity were made, the minority stockholder's equity would be 30.____

A. $15,600   B. $10,100   C. $12,200   D. $14,800

KEY (CORRECT ANSWERS)

1. B	11. D	21. A
2. A	12. B	22. C
3. D	13. A	23. D
4. B	14. B	24. C
5. A	15. A	25. D
6. C	16. D	26. A
7. A	17. B	27. A
8. D	18. C	28. B
9. C	19. C	29. B
10. D	20. B	30. C

TEST 3

DIRECTIONS: Each question or incomplete statement is followed by several suggested answers or completions. Select the one that BEST answers the question or completes the statement. *PRINT THE LETTER OF THE CORRECT ANSWER IN THE SPACE AT THE RIGHT.*

1. For the measurement of net income to be as realistic as possible, it is *desirable* that revenue be recognized at the point that 1._

   A. cash is collected from customers
   B. an order for merchandise or services is received from a customer
   C. a deposit or advance payment is received from a customer
   D. goods are delivered or services are rendered to customers

2. An accounting principle must receive substantial authoritative support to qualify as "generally accepted." Many organizations and agencies have been influential in the development of generally accepted accounting principles, but the MOST influential leadership has come from the 2._

   A. New York Stock Exchange
   B. American Institute of Certified Public Accountants
   C. Securities and Exchange Commission
   D. American Accounting Association

3. In which one of the following ways does the declaration and payment of a cash dividend affect corporate net income? It 3._

   A. does not affect net income
   B. reduces net income
   C. increases net income
   D. capitalizes net income

4. Under which one of the following headings of the corporate balance sheet should the liability for a dividend payable in stock appear? 4._

   A. Current Liabilities
   B. Long Term Liabilities
   C. Stockholders' Equity
   D. Current Assets

5. In which one of the following is "Working Capital" MOST likely to be found? 5._

   A. "Income Statement"
   B. "Analysis of Retained Earnings"
   C. "Computation of Cost of Capital"
   D. "Statement of Funds Provided and Applied"

6. Which of the following procedures is NOT generally mandatory in auditing a merchandising corporation? 6._

   A. Physical observation of inventory count
   B. Written circularization of accounts receivable
   C. Confirmation of bank balance
   D. Circularization of the stockholders

7. A company purchased office supplies during 2004 in the total amount of $1,400 and charged the entire amount to the asset account. An inventory of supplies taken on December 31, 2004 shows the cost of unused supplies to be $250. The entry to record this fact, assuming the books have not been closed, involves 7.____

A. credit to capital
B. debit to supplies expense
C. credit to supplies expense
D. debit to supplies on hand

8. A corporation's records show $600,000 (credit) in net sales, $200,000 (debit) in year-end accounts receivable, and $2,000 (debit) in Allowance for Bad Debts. The company's aged schedule of accounts receivable indicates a probable future loss from failure to collect year-end receivables in the amount of $6,000. Of the following, the MOST correct entry to adjust the Allowance for Bad Debts at year-end is 8.____

A. $1,000 credit
B. $4,000 credit
C. $8,000 debit
D. $8,000 credit

Questions 9-10.

A company commenced business in 2004 and purchased inventory as follows:

March	100 units @	$5	$ 500
June	300	6	1,800
October	200	7	1,400
November	500	7	3,500
December	100	6	600
TOTAL	1,200		$7,800

**Units sold in 2004 amounted to 900

9. Under the LIFO inventory principle, the value of the remaining inventory is 9.____

A. $1,700 B. $1,875 C. $2,145 D. $2,225

10. Under the FIFO inventory principle, the value of the remaining inventory is 10.____

A. $1,650 B. $1,875 C. $2,000 D. $2,025

11. When doing a trial balance, assume that, as a result of a single error, the total of the credit balances is greater than the total of the debit balances. Which one of the following single errors could NOT be the cause of this discrepancy? 11.____

A. Failure to post a debit
B. Posting a debit as a credit
C. Failure to post a credit
D. Posting a credit twice

Questions 12-13.

A and B are partners with capital balances of $20,000 and $30,000, respectively, at June 30, 2004, who share profits and losses, 40% and 60%, respectively. On July 1, 2004, C is to be admitted into the partnership under the following conditions:

- Partnership assets are to be revalued and increased by $10,000.
- C is to invest $40,000 but be credited for $30,000 while the remaining $10,000 is to be credited to A and B to compensate them for their preexisting goodwill.

12. After C is admitted and the proper entries are made, A's capital account will have a credit balance of 12.__

A. $24,500 B. $28,000 C. $30,200 D. $36,000

13. After the admission of C to the partnership, C's share of profits and losses is agreed upon at 20%. Assuming no other adjustments, the new percentage for profit and loss distribution to A will be 13.__

A. 18% B. 32% C. 36% D. 45%

14. A company reports as income for tax purposes $70,000 and its book income before the provision for income taxes is $100,000. Assuming a 50% tax rate, the *proper tax* expense to be recorded following tax allocation procedures is 14.__

A. $33,000 B. $40,000 C. $50,000 D. $60,000

15. The relationship between the total of cash and current receivables to total current liabilities is *commonly* referred to by accountants as the 15.__

A. acid-test ratio
B. cross-statement ratio
C. current ratio
D. R.O.I. ratio

16. On a statement of sources and application of funds, the depreciation expense is *normally* shown as a(n) 16.__

A. addition to operating income
B. subtraction from funds provided
C. addition to funds applied
D. reduction from operating income

17. Company A owns 100% of the capital stock of Company B and reports on a consolidated basis. During the year, Company A sold inventory to Company B at a profit of $100,000. One half of this inventory has been sold at year-end by Company B to the public. Which one of the following would be the MOST correct adjustment, if any, to make the consolidated retained earnings conform to generally accepted accounting principles? 17.__

A. Decrease by $50,000
B. Increase by $50,000
C. Increase by $100,000
D. No adjustment

18. X, Y and Z are partners with capital of $11,000, $12,000 and $4,500. X has a loan due from the partnership to him of $2,000. Profits and losses are shared in the ratio of 4:5:1 respectively. The partnership has paid off all outside liabilities, and its remaining assets consist of $9,000 in cash and $20,500 of accounts receivable. The partners agree to disburse the $9,000 to themselves in such a way that, even if one of the receivables is realized, no partner will have been overpaid.
Under these conditions, which of the following *most nearly* represents the amount to be paid to partner X? 18.__

A. $1,960 B. $3,200 C. $4,800 D. $5,000

19. R Company needs $2,000,000 to finance an expansion of plant facilities. The company expects to earn a return of 15% on this investment before considering the cost of capital or income taxes. The average income tax rate for the R Company is 40%. If the company raises the funds by issuing 6% bonds at face value, the earnings available to common stockholders after the new plant facilities are in operation may be expected to increase by 19.____

A. $65,000 B. $70,000 C. $108,000 D. $116,000

20. The budget for a given factory overhead cost was $150,000 for the year. The actual cost for the year was $125,000. Based on these facts, it can be said that the plant manager has done a better job than expected in controlling this cost if the cost is a 20.____

A. semi-variable cost
B. variable cost and actual production was 83-1/3% of budgeted production
C. semi-variable cost which includes a fixed element of $25,000 per period
D. variable cost and actual production was equal to budgeted production

21. The Home Office account on the books of the City Branch shows a credit balance of $15,000 at the end of a year and the City Branch account on the books of the Home Office shows a debit balance of $12,000. Of the following, the *most likely* reason for the discrepancy in the two accounts is that 21.____

A. merchandise shipped by the Home Office to the branch has not been recorded by the branch
B. the Home Office has not recorded a branch loss for the first quarter of the year
C. the branch has just mailed a check for $3,000 to the Home Office which has not yet been received by the Home Office
D. the Home Office has not yet recorded the branch profit for the first quarter of the year

22. The concept of matching costs and revenues means that 22.____

A. the expenses offset against revenues should be related to the same time period
B. revenues are at least as great as expenses on the average
C. revenues and expenses are equal
D. net income equals revenues minus expenses for the same earning period

23. If the inventory at the end of the current year is understated, and the error is not caught during the following year, the effect is to 23.____

A. *overstate* the income for the two-year period
B. *overstate* income this year and understate income next year
C. *understate* income this year and overstate income next year
D. *understate* income this year, with no effect on the income of the next year

KEY (CORRECT ANSWERS)

1.	D	11.	C	21.	D
2.	B	12.	B	22.	A
3.	A	13.	B	23.	C
4.	C	14.	C		
5.	D	15.	A		
6.	D	16.	A		
7.	B	17.	A		
8.	D	18.	C		
9.	A	19.	C		
10.	C	20.	D		

EXAMINATION SECTION
TEST 1

Directions: Each question or incomplete statement is followed by several suggested answers or completions. Select the one that BEST answers the question or completes the statement. *PRINT THE LETTER OF THE CORRECT ANSWER IN THE SPACE AT THE RIGHT.*

1) Which of following can usually NOT be accomplished through the use of an accounting system? 1. ______

A. Providing information to managers, owners, and other parties about solvency
B. Recording financial activity in monetary terms
C. Assuring profitability
D. Summarizing financial activities in a way that is useful

2) The main difference between financial accounting and managerial accounting is that financial accounting 2. ______

A. must be performed by a CPA
B. is performed for the purposes of internal control and oversight
C. is required by law
D. focuses on the information needs of external parties

3) Curry Landscaping purchased a concrete mixer with an invoice price of $8000. The terms of sale were 2/10. n/30, and Curry Landscaping paid within the discount period. Curry also paid a $100 delivery charge, a $130 installment charge, and $550 sales tax. What amount would be recorded as the cost of the equipment? 3. ______

A. $8250
B. $8390
C. $8620
D. $8780

4) In the ______________ method for reporting cash used in operating activities, the accountant lists the major classes of gross cash receipts and the gross cash payments from operations. 4. ______

A. double-entry
B. indirect
C. work sheet
D. direct

5) Unearned revenue is a(n) 5. ______

A. expense
B. revenue
C. liability
D. asset

6) A debit is used to record a decrease in a(n) 6. ______

I. asset
II. liability
III. owners' equity
IV. expense

A. I only
B. I and III
C. II, III and IV
D. I, II, III and IV

7) During its month's-end procedures at the end of July, the Blue Tang Inn neglects to include the adjusting entry to recognize interest owed to a lender. As a result, the 7. ______

A. expenses are understated and July 31 owners' equity understated
B. expenses are understated and July 31 assets overstated
C. net income is understated and July 31 assets overstated
D. net income is overstated and July 31 liabilities understated

8) The ________ method is used to classify individual receivables according to time elapsed from their due date. 8. ______

A. pro rata
B. aging
C. allowance
D. direct write-off

9) Credit is given on terms 2/10, n/30. This means that there will be a 9. ______

A. 2% cash discount if the amount is paid within 10 days, with the balance due in 30 days
B. 10% cash discount if the amount is paid within 2 days, with the balance due in 30 days
C. 30% discount if paid within 2 days
D. 30% discount if paid within 10 days

10) Which of the following accounts normally has a credit balance? 10. _____

A. Office equipment
B. Sales salaries expense
C. Sales salaries payable
D. Cash

11) Revenue earned on an account results in 11. _____

A. an increase in that asset, but a decrease in another asset
B. decreased assets and increased owners' equity
C. increased assets and increased owners' equity
D. decreased assets and decreased owners' equity

Questions 12-14 are based on the following information: Montana Ned's Golf Supply, at the end of last year, had merchandise costing $210,000 in inventory. During January of the current year, Montana Ned's bought merchandise costing $93,000, and sold merchandise for which it had paid a total of $81,000. Montana Ned's uses a perpetual inventory system.

12) What is the balance in the inventory account on January 31? 12. _____

A. $93,000
B. $210,000
C. $222,000
D. $384,000

13) What was the amount of costs transferred to from the inventory account to the cost of goods sold account during January? 13. _____

A. $12,000
B. $81,000
C. $93,000
D. $174,000

14) What was the total debited to Montana Ned's inventory account in January? 14. _____

A. $12,000
B. $81,000
C. $93,000
D. $174,000

15) Which of the following is TRUE about restrictions on retained earnings? 15. _____

A. They do not change overall retained earnings.
B. They increase overall retained earnings.
C. They decrease overall retained earnings.
D. They provide a cash fund for contingencies.

16) A(n) _______________ discount is a deduction from the invoice price of goods allowed if payment is made within a specified period of time. 16. _____

A. trade
B. early-bird
C. bulk
D. cash

17) A promissory note received from a customer in exchange for an account receivable would be classified as a(n) _______________ for the recipient 17. _____

A. note payable
B. account receivable
C. cash equivalent
D. note receivable

18) The balance of an unearned revenue account appears in 18. _____

A. a separate section of the income statement for revenue not yet earned
B. the liability section of the balance sheet
C. the income statement along with other revenue accounts
D. the balance sheet as a component of owners' equity

19) The maximum number of years a company is allowed to record a single intangible asset is 19. _____

A. 10
B. 17
C. 20
D. 35

20) Notes payable typically appear on the 20. _____

A. income statement
B. balance sheet
C. statement of cash flows
D. statement of retained earnings

21) The most likely reason why a corporation's stock trades at a very high price/earnings ratio is that 21. _____

A. the corporation has several classes of stock outstanding
B. the corporation is very large and considered a low risk
C. investors expect the corporation to have higher earnings in the future
D. investors intend to sell short

22) WorldWater has total current liabilities of $70,000. After employees are paid $10,000 of the wages payable to the company owed from last year, current liabilities would be 22. _____

A. $60,000
B. $70,000
C. $75,000
D. $80,000

23) Which of the following is included in a company's cash flow from financing activities? 23. _____

A. Cash received from the issue of common stock
B. Cash paid for employee salaries
C. Cash paid for income taxes
D. Cash paid for the purchase of capital equipment

24) Which of the following is a current liability? 24. _____

A. Buildings used in business operations
B. Wages payable
C. Office supplies
D. Long-term note payable

25) An end-of-period inventory amount that is incorrectly reported can result in misstated 25. _____

I. net income
II. gross profits
III. current assets
IV. cost of goods sold

A. I and II
B. I, II and III
C. III and IV
D. I, II, III and IV

KEY (CORRECT ANSWERS)

1. C
2. D
3. C
4. D
5. C

6. C
7. D
8. B
9. A
10. C

11. C
12. C
13. B
14. C
15. A

16. D
17. D
18. B
19. C
20. B

21. C
22. A
23. A
24. B
25. D

TEST 2

Directions: Each question or incomplete statement is followed by several suggested answers or completions. Select the one that BEST answers the question or completes the statement. *PRINT THE LETTER OF THE CORRECT ANSWER IN THE SPACE AT THE RIGHT.*

1) Sales for the year were $200,000, and the cost of sales was $120,000. If the average inventory for the year was $40,000, what was the inventory turnover? 1. ______

A. 1.67
B. 3
C. 3.67
D. 5

2) Chuzzlewit Enterprises sold equipment for $30,000. The cost was $70,000, and the equipment had accumulated depreciation of $50,000 at the time of the sale. If the is using the direct method, the amount of __________ would be entered for this transaction in the operating section of the cash flow statement. 2. ______

A. $(10,000)
B. 0 (no entry)
C. $10,000
D. $30,000

3) An accountant is preparing a bank reconciliation. A service charge shown on the bank statement should be 3. ______

A. deducted from the balance in the depositor's records
B. deducted from the balance in the bank statement
C. added to the balance in the depositor's records
D. added to the balance in the depositor's records

4) For several years, the net income of Stanton, Inc. has been rising as a percentage of the company's net sales. Analysts would usually interpret this to mean that 4. ______

A. the portion of the company's assets that are financed on credit is decreasing
B. net sales are increasing faster than inflation
C. sales volume has been decreasing
D. the company has been successfully controlling expenses

5) Which of the following occurs when a company issues a stock dividend? 5. ______

A. Earned capital increases and contributed capital decreases.
B. Earned capital decreases and contributed capital increases.
C. Total shareholder equity increases.
D. Total shareholder equity decreases.

6) Harlan uses a perpetual inventory system. Its beginning inventory for the current year was 10 units, purchased at a cost of $10 each. During the current year Harlan purchased 20 units at $12 each. 12 units are sold in the current year. Using the first-in, first-out (FIFO) method, calculate the total cost of the 12 units that were sold. 6. ______

A. $116
B. $120
C. $124
D. $130

7) Bad debt expense can be estimated by using the ________________ method. 7. ______

I. percent of accounts receivable
II. percent of sales
III. allowance
IV. aging of accounts receivable

A. I only
B. I and II
C. III only
D. I, II, III and IV

8) Accelerated methods of depreciation include the ________________ method. 8. ______

I. sum-of-the-years'-digits
II. double declining balance
III. production units
IV. straight-line

A. I and II
B. II and III
C. I, III and IV
D. I, II, III and IV

Questions 9 and 10 refer to the following: Bougainville Enterprises reports the following results in its financial statements.

	2010	2009	2008
Net Sales	$2.5 million	$2.05 million	$1.9 million
Accounts Receivable, ending	$175,000	$167,000	$165,000

9) For 2009, Bougainville's accounts receivable turnover rate was 9. ______

A. 12.3
B. 14.6
C. 16.5
D. 17.8

10) For 2010, Bougainville's accounts receivable turnover rate was 10. ______

A. 12.3
B. 14.6
C. 16.5
D. 17.8

11) Cash equivalents include 11. ______

A. money orders
B. 6-month certificates of deposit
C. checking accounts
D. short-term liquid investments

12) Rent expense typically appears on the 12. ______

A. income statement
B. statement of retained earnings
C. statement of cash flows
D. balance sheet

13) Hexagon Corporation has 1,000 shares of $100 par value preferred stock, and $25,000 shares of common stock outstanding. Its total stockholders' equity is $500,000. The book value per common share is 13. ______

A. $15
B. $16
C. $18.25
D. $20

14) Which of the following items would NOT be added to the balance per book? 14. _____

A. A deposit in transit
B. A customer note collected by the bank
C. Interest earned on an account
D. A check for $100 recorded as $100 in the check register

15) The ____________ ratio is a type of profitability ratio. 15. _____

A. current
B. quick
C. accounts receivable turnover
D. return on assets

16) The concept of adequate disclosure means that financial statements should be accompanied by an information for the statements to be interpreted properly. Examples of these notations include 16. _____

I. due dates of major liabilities
II. accounting methods and policies
III. significant events occurring between the time the balance sheet was recorded and the financial statements were issued
IV. name of the company's financial institution

A. I and II
B. I, II and III
C. III only
D. I, II, III and IV

17) What is the term used to describe horizontal addition or subtraction across columns? 17. _____

A. Cross-footing
B. Keying
C. Journalizing
D. Footing

18) The ______________ method is recommended for amortization of discounts or premiums. 18. _____

A. double declining balance
B. straight-line
C. effective interest
D. sum-of-the-years'-digits

19. L. Eron and A. Pilott are partners who share income and losses in the ratio of 3:2, respectively. The balance in the Profit and Loss account on December 31, 2004, prior to distribution to the partners, is $20,800. Before distributing any profits to the partnership in the agreed ratio, L. Eron is to be given credit for interest on his loan of $60,000, outstanding for the entire year, at 6% per annum. A. Pilott is to receive a bonus of 10% of the net income over $5,100, after deducting the bonus to himself and the interest to L. Eron. Giving consideration to all the above information, the total amount of net income to be credited to A. Pilott is 19.____

A. $8,320 B. $2,080 C. $7,540 D. $15,700

Questions 20-21.

Schneider and Samuels are partners with capital balances on December 31, 2004 of $15,000 and $25,000, respectively. They share profits in a ratio of 2:1.

Goroff is to be admitted to the partnership. He agrees to be admitted as a partner with a cash investment to give him a one-third interest in the capital and profits of the business. All the parties agree that the good will to be granted to Goroff should be valued at $6,000.

20. The required cash to cover Goroff's investment in a business partnership according to the terms stated is 20.____

A. $20,000 B. $14,000 C. $6,000 D. $25,000

21. After his cash investment, and all other initial entries, the credit to Goroff's Capital account is 21.____

A. $20,000 B. $14,000 C. $6,000 D. $25,000

22. The Marlin Corp. sold 7,800 units of its product at $25 per unit and suffered a net loss for its calendar year ending December 31, 2003 of $2,000.
The fixed expenses amounted to $80,000 and the variable expenses $117,000. The Marlin Corp. believes that by expending $20,000 in an advertising campaign, it could increase its sales, retaining the $25 per unit selling price, to generate a profit.
Assuming the above facts, the sales revenue for 2003 reflecting the break-even point is 22.____

A. $195,000 B. $217,000 C. $250,000 D. $300,000

23. The Anide Corp., which keeps its books on the accrual basis, had the following transactions for its calendar year ending December 31, 2004: 23.____
- April 15, 2004 - Authorized the issuance of $3,000,000 of 5.5%, 20 year bonds, dated May 1, 2004. Interest to be paid November 1 and May 1.
- June 1, 2004 - Sold the entire issue at $2,964,150 plus accrued interest.
- November 1, 2004 - Paid the interest due.

The interest expense for the calendar year ending December 31, 2004 is

A. $85,000 B. $165,000 C. $110,000 D. $97,300

Questions 24-26.

The following information was taken from a worksheet that was used in the preparation of the balance sheet and the profit and loss statement of the Hott Company for 2004:

The Balance Sheet Contained	Amount
Travel Expense Unpaid	$995
Legal and Collection Fees - Prepaid in Advance	672
Interest Received in Advance	469

The Profit and Loss Statement Contained	Amount
Travel Expenses	$7,343
Legal and Collection Fees	5,461
Interest Income	3,114

The proper adjusting and closing entries were made on the books of the company by the accountant and the described information was reported on the financial statements. The books are kept on an accrual basis.

On the basis of the above facts, the balance in each of the following accounts in the trial balance, *before adjusting and closing entries were made,* was as follows:

24. Travel Expense Account 24._

A. $8,338 B. $7,343 C. $6,348 D. $995

25. Legal and Collection Fees Account 25._

A. $672 B. $4,789 C. $5,461 D. $6,133

26. Interest Income Account 26._

A. $3,583 B. $3,114 C. $2,645 D. $469

Questions 27-28.

The following is the stockholder's equity section of a corporation:

Preferred Stock (7%, cumulative, non-participating, $100 par value, 5,000 shares issued and outstanding)	$ 500,000
Common Stock ($1.00 par value, 500,000 issued and outstanding)	500,000
	1,000,000
Deficit	(40,000)
	$ 960,000

27. Assuming two years' dividends in arrears on the preferred stock, the book value per share of common stock is 27._

A. 78¢ B. 80¢ C. 63¢ D. 94¢

KEY (CORRECT ANSWERS)

1. B
2. B
3. A
4. D
5. B

6. C
7. D
8. A
9. A
10. B

11. D
12. A
13. B
14. A
15. D

16. B
17. A
18. C
19. D
20. C

21. A
22. B
23. C
24. B
25. B

TEST 3

Directions: Each question or incomplete statement is followed by several suggested answers or completions. Select the one that BEST answers the question or completes the statement. *PRINT THE LETTER OF THE CORRECT ANSWER IN THE SPACE AT THE RIGHT.*

1) ________________ stock is a term that refers to shares of a corporation's stock that have been issued and reacquired, but not canceled. 1. ______

A. Cumulative preferred
B. No-par
C. Non-cumulative preferred
D. Treasury

2) The paid-in capital section of a balance sheet includes each of the following, EXCEPT 2. ______

A. retained earnings
B. preferred stock
C. common stock
D. common stock subscribed

3) Chubby Taxi just purchased a new cab. The initial cost would include each of the following, EXCEPT 3. ______

A. sales tax
B. purchase price
C. the installation of air conditioning before using the cab
D. first year's liability insurance

4) During a period of rising costs, the ________________ method of inventory valuation method yields the lowest reported net income. 4. ______

A. last in, first out (LIFO)
B. first in, first out (FIFO)
C. weighted-average
D. average cost

5) Unearned revenues are 5. ______

A. any increases to owners' equity
B. revenues that have been earned and received, but not deposited
C. revenues that have been earned, but not yet collected
D. liabilities that are created by advance payments for goods or services

6) Red Max Corporation had a credit balance in the allowance for doubtful accounts of $200 at the start of the current year. During the year, a provision of 2% of sales was made for uncollectible accounts. Sales for the year were $500,000 and $8000 of accounts receivable were written off as worthless. Also, no recoveries of accounts previously written off were made during the year. The year-end financial statement would show a 6. ______

A. $10,000 credit balance in the allowance for doubtful accounts
B. $2000 credit balance in the allowance for doubtful accounts
C. $10,200 bad debts expense
D. $9800 bad debts expense

7) A company's current assets include 7. ______

I. Merchandise inventory
II. Prepaid expenses
III. Accounts receivable
IV. Land held for future plant expansion

A. I and II
B. II and III
C. I, II, and III
D. I, II, III and IV

8) The maturity value of a note is the 8. ______

A. face value plus any stated interest
B. discounted value of the note
C. par value less the discount
D. principal less the discount

9) A company can retire bonds by 9. ______

I. converting them to stock for the holders
II. paying off the bonds at maturity.
III. purchasing the bonds on the open market
IV. exercising a call option

A. I and II
B. II and III
C. III only
D. I, II, III and IV

10) Within the past year, Wildcat Oil purchased and then sold land containing 15 million gallons of oil for $4,875,000. While it owned the land, Wildcat pumped and sold 789,000 gallons of oil. The depletion expense for the year would be 10. _____

A. $97,500
B. $181,995
C. $256,425
D. $301,667

11) Genetico has sold land for cash at a price greater than its cost. Each of the following is a result of this transaction, EXCEPT that 11. _____

A. owners' equity is increased
B. total assets are unaffected
C. cash is increased
D. liabilities are unaffected

12) Which of the following is a financing activity? 12. _____

A. Signing a note payable in exchange for cash
B. Settling an account payable with cash
C. Purchasing a warehouse in exchange for shares of stock
D. Selling land for cash

13) The Kasnoff Group adjusts its accounts at the end of the year for consulting services of $9000 performed for a client in December that have not yet been collected in cash. This adjustment will result in a $9000 13. _____

A. decrease in both liabilities and owners' equity
B. increase in both assets and liabilities
C. increase in both assets and owners' equity
D. decrease in both assets and liabilities

14) Which of the following would be recorded as a contingent liability? 14. _____

A. Debt guarantees
B. Warranty on products sold
C. Unearned revenues
D. Property taxes payable

15) "Mark to market" is the balance sheet valuation standard for 15. _____

A. investments in capital stock of any corporation
B. stockholders' equity of any publicly traded corporation
C. investments in all financial assets
D. investments in marketable securities

16) Frogpond Enterprises normally sells it product for $20 each, which involves a profit margin of 25%. The selling price has fallen to $15. Frogpond's current inventory is 200 units, purchased at $16 each. Replacement cost is not $13 per unit. Using the lower of cost or market, Frogpond's inventory is now valued at 16. _____

A. $2500
B. $2550
C. $2600
D. $2700

17) According to the concept of present value, a bond that paid a below market rate would sell at a price 17. _____

A. below its maturity value
B. equal to its maturity value
C. above its maturity value
D. that may vary in accordance with the issuer's credit rating

Questions 18-20 are based on the following information: Aquitaine's stockholders earn $6 per share and $2 dividends annually on stocks that are priced at $24 per share. The common shareholders' equity is $600,000, and the shares of common stock outstanding amount to $1.2 million.

18) Aquitaine's P/E ratio is 18. _____

A. 0.33
B. 2
C. 3
D. 4

19) Aquitaine's dividend yield is 19. _____

A. 0.083
B. 0.33
C. 1.2
D. 3

20) The book value per share of Aquitaine stock is 20. _____

A. 0.25
B. 0.5
C. 2
D. 4

21) Which of the following would cause a temporary difference between taxable and pretax accounting income? 21. ____

A. Life insurance benefits paid upon the death of an executive officer
B. Investment expenses incurred to generate tax-exempt income
C. The deduction of dividends received
D. The use of MACRS to depreciate equipment

22) If a bond has a par value of $1000 and the market price is $989.10, the bond is selling at 22. ____

A. a discount
B. the coupon rate
C. a premium
D. face value

23) If revenues are less than expenses during a given accounting period, 23. ____

I. the income statement will show a net loss
II. assets will decrease more than liabilities
III. owners' equity will decrease more than assets
IV. the cash account will decrease

A. I only
B. I and II
C. I, II, and III
D. I, II, III and IV

24) Klaxon receives a 10%, 90-day note for $1500. The total interest on the note is 24. ____

A. $37.50
B. $50
C. $75
D. $87.50

25) STX International and Holoport each makes and sells telecommunications equipment. Holoport uses the first-in, first-out (FIFO) method for valuing inventory, and STX uses last-in, first-out (FIFO). Due to technological innovations and improvements, the cost of making telecommunications equipment has decreased over the past several years. Based on these assumptions, STX International—over the past several years—would be more likely to 25. _____

A. have a lower inventory value on the year-end balance sheet
B. report a higher gross margin on the income statement
C. have a higher amount of owners' equity
D. pay less in income taxes

KEY (CORRECT ANSWERS)

1. D
2. A
3. D
4. A
5. D

6. B
7. C
8. A
9. D
10. C

11. B
12. A
13. C
14. A
15. D

16. C
17. A
18. D
19. A
20. B

21. D
22. A
23. A
24. A
25. C

TEST 4

Directions: Each question or incomplete statement is followed by several suggested answers or completions. Select the one that BEST answers the question or completes the statement. *PRINT THE LETTER OF THE CORRECT ANSWER IN THE SPACE AT THE RIGHT.*

1) Which of the following is NOT a short-term liquidity ratio? 1. ______

A. Defensive interval
B. Inventory turnover
C. Accounts receivable turnover
D. Debt to total assets

2) What is the term for the original cost of an asset less its accumulated depreciation? 2. ______

A. Net present value
B. Replacement cost
C. Current value
D. Book value

3) Starlingcourt, which has total assets of $400,000, borrows $80,000 from the bank. Which of the following is true? 3. ______

A. Owners' equity remains unchanged.
B. Owners' equity increases by $80,000.
C. Owners' equity decreases by $80,000
D. Total assets are now $320,000

4) Of the following steps in the accounting cycle, which is performed the LATEST in the process? 4. ______

A. Adjusting accounts
B. Preparing financial statements
C. Preparing the adjusted trial balance
D. Posting

5) When a business pays a liability with cash, the accountant should record the decrease in 5. ______

A. cash as a debit
B. accounts receivable as a credit
C. accounts receivable as a debit
D. accounts payable as a debit

6) Bettancourt issues 9%, 20-year bonds with a par value of $750,000. The current market rate is 9%. The total amount of interest owed to bondholders for each semiannual interest payment is 6. ______

A. $33,750
B. $67,500
C. $101,250
D. $135,000

7) The statement of cash flows helps in the analysis of the 7. ______

I. differences between net income and net operating cash flow
II. means used to finance investing activities
III. source of cash for debt repayment
IV. source of cash for plant expansion

A. I and II
B. II and III
C. III only
D. I, II, III and IV

8) A company's quick ratio is 8. ______

A. in indication of the time a company takes to pay its short-term creditors
B. never larger than its current ratio on the same day
C. determined by dividing current assets by current liabilities, excluding accounts payable for inventory purchases
D. an indication of how quickly a company converts its current assets to cash.

9) Hazbin Corporation has assets of $100,000, liabilities of $10,000, and equity of $90,000. It buys office equipment on credit for $5,000. Effects of this transaction include a 9. ______

I. $5000 increase in liabilities
II. $5000 increase in assets
III. $5000 increase in equity
IV. $5000 decrease in equity

A. I only
B. I and II
C. I, II and III
D. IV only

10) Pet Palace used the retail method to estimate its ending inventory in its monthly financial statements. On November 30, goods available for sale during the month had cost $20,000 and had been given retail prices of $50,000. Sales for the month amounted to $30,000. The estimated ending inventory to appear in the November 30 balance sheet is 10. _____

A. $8000
B. $12,000
C. $20,000
D. $38,000

11) The double-entry system of accounting requires that 11. _____

A. the total number of debit entries must equal the number of credit entries
B. debits must equal credits when the trial balance is prepared
C. two entries must be made for each transaction
D. the dollar amount of debit items must equal the dollar amount of credit items for each journal entry

Questions 12-14 refer to the information below.

Ukraine Appliance Outlet uses a periodic inventory system. It sold 900 kitchen mixers in the last year. The inventory data was as follows:

1/1	Balance	100 mixers @ $70.00	=$ 7000
3/6	Bought	500 mixers @ $80.00	=$40,000
7/15	Bought	400 mixers @ $90.00	=$36,000
10/23	Bought	400 mixers @$100.00	=$40,000
Inventory available:		1400 mixers	$123,000

12) Under the first-in, first-out (FIFO) method, ending inventory is 12. _____

A. $35,000
B. $39,000
C. $49,000
D. $50,000

13) Under the last-in, last-out (LIFO) method, ending inventory is 13. _____

A. $35,000
B. $39,000
C. $49,000
D. $50,000

14) Cost of goods sold under the last-in, last-out (LIFO) method is 14. _____

A. $71,000
B. $74,000
C. $84,000
D. $87,000

15) A company that sold machinery during an accounting period would record the transaction as a(n) 15. _____

A. financing activity inflow
B. financing activity outflow
C. investing activity inflow
D. investing activity outflow

16) Ugolino Enterprises had net sales of $4.235 billion and ending accounts receivable of $775 million, resulting in __________ days' sales uncollected. 16. _____

A. 34.7
B. 65.2
C. 66.8
D. 81.8

17) The _______________ principle requires that financial statement information be based on costs incurred in business transactions, and requires assets and services to be recorded initially at the cash or cash-equivalent amount given in exchange. 17. _____

A. cost
B. business entity
C. going-concern
D. realization

18) Carlson Corporation earns a rate of return on common stockholders' equity of 14%. The company will cause the rate of return to increase if it 18. _____

A. increases its P/E ratio
B. increases the size of the cash dividend paid on common stock
C. increases the market price of its stock
D. issues 10% bonds and invests the proceeds to earn 12%

19) An adjusting entry for accrued revenues will increase the __________ account. 19. _____

I. revenue
II. expense
III. asset
IV. liability

A. I only
B. I and III
C. II and IV
D. IV only

20) Which of the following would be recorded as an estimated liability? 20. _____

A. Accounts payable
B. Payroll taxes payable
C. Income taxes payable
D. Lawsuit against the company

21) Stabile Corporation has the following information available at year's end: 21. _____

Cost of Goods Sold	$175,000
Net Credit Sales	$250,000
Beginning inventory	$40,000
Beginning accounts receivable	$15,000
Ending inventory	$50,000
Ending accounts receivable	$45,000

Stabile's inventory turnover ratio for the year was

A. 0.31
B. 3.5
C. 3.89
D. 5.21

22) Liquidating dividends are distributed when 22. _____

A. a company pays dividends in excess of its retained earnings
B. the company is extremely profitable
C. the dividends are in arrears
D. there are both common and preferred dividends

23) The gross margin method of estimating ending inventory 23. _____

A. is the most accurate estimating method
B. uses the current relationship between goods available for sale and retail prices
C. uses the historical average gross margin percent
D. uses only the most recent gross margin percent

24) Hafkemeyer Irrigation, which uses a perpetual inventory system, had a beginning inventory of 5 units, costing $20 each. During the year it made two purchases: the first for 10 units at $22 each and the second for 6 units at $25 each. 8 units were sold for $350 retail. Using the last-in, first-out (LIFO) method, calculate the value of the inventory after these 8 sales were made. 24. _____

A. $276
B. $288
C. $296
D. $304

25) Cash includes 25. _____

I. deposits in checking and savings accounts
II. any item that a bank customarily accepts for immediate deposit
III. IOUs
IV. notes receivable

A. I only
B. I and II
C. I, II and III
D. I, II, III and IV

KEY (CORRECT ANSWERS)

1. D
2. D
3. A
4. B
5. D

6. A
7. D
8. B
9. B
10. A

11. D
12. C
13. B
14. C
15. C

16. C
17. A
18. D
19. B
20. C

21. C
22. A
23. C
24. C
25. B

EXAMINATION SECTION
TEST 1

DIRECTIONS: Each question or incomplete statement is followed by several suggested answers or completions. Select the one that BEST answers the question or completes the statement. *PRINT THE LETTER OF THE CORRECT ANSWER IN THE SPACE AT THE RIGHT.*

Questions 1-3.

DIRECTIONS: Questions 1 through 3 are to be answered on the basis of the following information.

Wayland Company's December 31 year-end financial statements contained the following errors:

	December 31, 2004	December 31, 2005
Ending inventory	$2,000 understated	$1,800 overstated
Depreciation expense	$400 understated	

An insurance premium of $1,800 was prepaid in 2004 covering the years 2004, 2005, and 2006. The entire amount was charged to expense in 2004. In addition, on December 31, 2005, fully depreciated machinery was sold for $3,200 cash, but the sale was not recorded until 2006. There were no other errors during 2004 or 2005, and no corrections have been made for any of the errors. (Ignore income tax considerations.)

1. What is the total effect of the errors on 2005 net income? Net income 1.____
   A. overstated by $600 B. overstated by $700
   C. understated by $900 D. overstated by $1,100

2. What is the total effect of the errors on the amount of Wayland's working capital at December 31, 2005? 2.____
   Working capital
   A. overstated by $1,000 B. understated by $1,400
   C. understated by $1,500 D. understated by $1,900

3. What is the total effect of the errors on the balance of Wayland's retained earnings at December 31, 2005? 3.____
   Retained earnings
   A. understated by $900 B. understated by $1,500
   C. understated by $1,700 D. overstated by $1,900

4. How should the gain or loss from an event or transaction that meets the criteria for infrequent occurrence but not unusual nature be disclosed? 4.____
   A. Separately in the earnings statement immediately after earnings from continuing operations
   B. On a net-of-tax basis in the earnings statement immediately after earnings from continuing operations

C. As an extraordinary item and treated accordingly in the earnings statement
D. Separately in the earnings statement as a component of earnings from continuing operations

5. Which of the following reporting practices is permissible for interim financial reporting? 5.____
A. Use of the gross-profit method for interim inventory pricing
B. Use of the direct-costing method for determining manufacturing inventories
C. Deferral of unplanned variances under a standard-cost system until year-end
D. Deferral of inventory market declines until year-end

6. Minimum disclosure requirements for companies issuing interim financial information would include which of the following? 6.____
A. An interim statement of financial position and statement of changes in financial position
B. Primary and fully diluted earnings per share data for each period presented
C. Sales and cost of goods sold for the current quarter and the current year-to-date
D. The contribution margin by product line for the current quarter and the current year-to-date

7. How should any compensation involved in a compensatory employee stock option plan be expensed? 7.____
A. In the period in which the options are exercised
B. In the period containing the measurement date
C. Proportionately in the time interval between the measurement date and the exercise date
D. In the period(s) in which related services are performed

8. The measurement date in accounting for stock issued to employees in compensatory stock option plans is the 8.____
A. date on which options are granted to specified employees
B. earliest date on which both the number of shares to be issued and option price are known
C. date on which the options are exercised by the employees
D. date the corporation foregoes alternative use of the shares to be sold under option

9. A planned factory expansion project has an estimated initial cost of $800,000. Using a discount rate of 20%, the present value of future cost savings from the expansion is $843,000. To yield exactly a 20% time-adjusted rate of return, the actual investment cost CANNOT exceed the $800,000 estimate by more than 9.____
A. $160,000 B. $20,000 C. $43,000 D. $1,075

Questions 10-11.

DIRECTIONS: Questions 10 and 11 are to be answered on the basis of the following information.

Standard costs and other data for two component parts used by Andes Electronics are presented below:

	Part A4	Part B5
Direct material	$ .40	$ 8.00
Direct labor	1.00	4.70
Factory overhead	4.00	2.00
Unit standard cost	$5.40	$14.70
Units needed per year	6,000	8,000
Machine hours per unit	4	2
Unit cost if purchased	$5.00	$15.00

In past years, Andes has manufactured all of its required components; however, in 2005 only 30,000 hours of otherwise idle machine time can be devoted to the production of components. Accordingly, some of the parts must be purchased from outside suppliers. In producing parts, factory overhead is applied at $1.00 per standard machine hour. Fixed capacity costs, which will not be affected by any make-buy decision, represent 60% of the applied overhead.

10. The 30,000 hours of available machine time are to be scheduled so that Andes realizes maximum potential cost savings. 10.____
The relevant unit production costs which should be considered in the decision to schedule machine time are _____ for A4 and _____ for B5.
A. $5.40; $14.70
B. $5.00; $15.00
C. $1.40; $12.70
D. $3.00; $13.50

11. If the allocation of machine time is based upon potential cost savings per machine hour, then Andes should produce _____ units of A4 and _____ units of B5. 11.____
A. 3,500; 8,000
B. 6,000; 8,000
C. 6,000; 3,000
D. no; 8,000

Questions 12-17.

DIRECTIONS: Questions 12 through 17 deal with the calculation of ratios and the determination of other factors considered important in analysis of financial statements. Prior to the occurrence of the independent events described below, the corporation concerned had current and quick ratios in excess of one to one and reported a net income (as opposed to a loss) for the period just ended. Income tax effects of the events are to be ignored. The corporation had only one class of shares outstanding.

12. The effect of recording a 100% stock dividend would be to 12.___
   A. decrease the current ratio, decrease working capital, and decrease book value per share
   B. leave inventory turnover unaffected, decrease working capital, and decrease book value per share
   C. leave working capital unaffected, decrease earnings per share, and decrease book value per share
   D. leave working capital unaffected, decrease earnings per share, and decrease the debt to equity ratio

13. Recording the payment (as distinguished from the declaration) of a cash dividend whose declaration was already recorded will 13.___
   A. increase the current ratio but have no effect on working capital
   B. decrease both the current ratio and working capital
   C. increase both the current ratio and working capital
   D. have no effect on the current ratio or earnings per share

14. What would be the effect on book value per share and earnings per share if the corporation purchased its own shares in the open market at a price greater than book value per share? 14.___
   A. No effect on book value per share but increase earnings per share
   B. Increase both book value per share and earnings per share
   C. Decrease both book value per share and earnings per share
   D. Decrease book value per share and increase earnings per share

15. If the corporation were to increase the extent to which it successfully *traded on the equity*, this fact would likely be manifested in a combination of facts that its 15.___
   A. ratio of owners' equity to total assets decreased while its ratio of net income to owners' equity increased
   B. book value and earnings per share decreased
   C. working capital decreased while its current ratio increased
   D. asset turnover and return on sales both decreased

16. The corporation exercises control over an affiliate in which it holds a 40% common stock interest. If its affiliate completed a fiscal year profitably but paid no dividends, how would this affect the investor corporation? 16.___
   A. Result in an increased current ratio
   B. Result in increased earnings per share
   C. Increase several turnover ratios
   D. Decrease book value per share

17. What would be the MOST probable cause of an increase in the rate of inventory turnover while the rate of receivables turnover decreased when compared with the prior period? 17.___
   A. Sales volume has changed markedly.
   B. Investment in inventory has decreased while investment in receivables has increased.
   C. Investment in inventory has increased while investment in receivables has decreased.
   D. The corporation has shortened the credit period for customers (tightened credit terms).

Questions 18-19.

DIRECTIONS: Questions 18 and 19 are to be answered on the basis of the following information.

Comparative balance sheets are presented for Shelly, Inc., a calendar-year company.

	December 31,	
	2005	2004
	Dr. (Cr)	Dr. (Cr)
Current assets	$237,000	$160,000
Equipment	615,000	600,000
Accumulated depreciation	(218,000)	(210,000)
Goodwill	240,000	250,000
	$874,000	$800,000
Current liabilities	$(180,000)	$(80,000)
Bonds payable	(200,000)	(300,000)
Discount on bonds	-	4,000
Common stock	(550,000)	(550,000)
Retained earnings	56,000	126,000
	$(874,000)	$(800,000)

You have discovered the following facts:
- During 2005, Shelly sold at no gain or loss equipment with a book value of $38,000 and purchased new equipment costing $75,000.
- During 2005, bonds with a face value of $100,000 were extinguished. They were not current liabilities prior to their extinguishment.
- Retained earnings was affected only by the 2005 net income or loss.

18. How much working capital was provided by operations during 2005 (net income adjusted for items not affecting working capital)? 18.___
   A. $104,000 B. $106,000 C. $110,000 D. $114,000

19. Assume that $100,000 face value of bonds became current at December 31, 2005, to be repaid in early 2006. What should be the change in working capital under this assumption after considering all changes in financial position? 19.___

A. $23,000 increase
B. $23,000 decrease
C. $123,000 increase
D. $123,000 decrease

20. Pelham Bros. manufactures two products, A and B. Each product must be processed in each of three departments: machining, assembling, and finishing. The hours needed to produce one unit of product per department and the maximum possible hours per department follow: 20.___

Department	Production Hours Per Unit A	Production Hours Per Unit B	Maximum Capacity In Hours
Machining	2	1	420
Assembling	2	2	500
Finishing	2	3	600

Other restrictions follow: A > 50
B > 50

The objective function is to maximize profits where profit = $4A + $2B.
Given the objective and constraints, what is the MOST profitable number of units of A and B, respectively, to manufacture?

A. 150 and 100
B. 165 and 90
C. 170 and 80
D. 200 and 50

KEY (CORRECT ANSWERS)

1. D	11. A
2. D	12. C
3. B	13. A
4. D	14. D
5. A	15. A
6. B	16. B
7. D	17. B
8. B	18. D
9. C	19. D
10. D	20. C

TEST 2

DIRECTIONS: Each question or incomplete statement is followed by several suggested answers or completions. Select the one that BEST answers the question or completes the statement. *PRINT THE LETTER OF THE CORRECT ANSWER IN THE SPACE AT THE RIGHT.*

Questions 1-4.

DIRECTIONS: Questions 1 through 4 are to be answered on the basis of the following information.

Gary Manufacturing Company buys zeon for $.80 a gallon. At the end of processing in Department 1, zeon splits off into products A, B, and C. Product A is sold at the split-off point, with no further processing. Products B and C require further processing before they can be sold; product B is processed in Department 2, and product C is processed in Department 3. Following is a summary of costs and other related data for the year ended June 30, 2005.

	Department		
	1	2	3
Cost of zeon	$96,000	-	-
Direct labor	$14,000	$45,000	$65,000
Manufacturing overhead	$10,000	$21,000	$49,000

	Products		
	A	B	C
Gallons sold	20,000	30,000	45,000
Gallons on hand at 6/30/05	10,000	-	15,000
Sales in dollars	$30,000	$96,000	$141,750

There were no inventories on hand at July 1, 2004, and there was no zeon on hand at June 30, 2005. All gallons on hand at June 30, 2005 were complete as to processing. There were no manufacturing-overhead variances. Gary uses the relative-sales-value method of allocating joint costs.

1. For allocating joint costs, the relative sales value of product A for the year ended June 30, 2005 would be 1.____
   A. $30,000 B. $45,000 C. $21,000 D. $6,000

2. The joint costs for the year ended June 30, 2005 to be allocated are 2.____
   A. $300,000 B. $95,000 C. $120,000 D. $96,000

3. The cost of product B sold for the year ended June 30, 2005 is 3.____
   A. $90,000 B. $66,000 C. $88,857 D. $96,000

4. The value of the ending inventory for product A is 4.____
A. $24,000 B. $12,000 C. $8,000 D. $13,333

5. The operations of a public library receiving the majority of its support from property taxes levied for that purpose should be accounted for in 5.____
A. the general fund
B. a special revenue fund
C. an enterprise fund
D. an intragovernmental service fund
E. none of the above

6. The liability for general obligation bonds issued for the benefit of a municipal electric company and serviced by its earnings should be recorded in 6.____
A. an enterprise fund
B. the general fund
C. an enterprise fund and the general long-term debt group
D. an enterprise fund and disclosed in a footnote in the statement of general long-term debt
E. none of the above

7. The liability for special assessment bonds which carry a secondary pledge of a municipality's general credit should be recorded in a(n) 7.____
A. enterprise fund
B. special revenue fund and general long-term debt group
C. special assessment fund and the general long-term debt group
D. a special assessment fund and disclosed in a footnote in the statement of general long-term debt
E. none of the above

8. The proceeds of a federal grant made to assist in financing the future construction of an adult training center should be recorded in 8.____
A. the general fund
B. a special revenue fund
C. a capital projects fund
D. a special assessment fund
E. none of the above

9. The account, Equity in Assigned Accounts Receivable, should be classified as a(n) 9.____
A. asset B. contra-asset
C. liability D. contra-liability

10. If a company converted a short-term note payable into a long-term note payable, this transaction would 10.____
A. decrease only working capital
B. decrease both working capital and the current ratio
C. increase only working capital
D. increase both working capital and the current ratio

11. If an industrial firm uses the absorption costing method for assigning cost to its inventories and the units-of-production method for computing depreciation on its only plant asset, factory machinery, the credit to accumulated depreciation from period to period during the life of the asset will 11.___

A. be constant
B. vary with unit sales
C. vary with sales revenue
D. vary with production

12. A company places orders for inventory with its suppliers for a certain item for which the order size is determined in advance as: 12.___

$$\text{Order Size} = \sqrt{\frac{2 \times \frac{\text{Cost to Place}}{\text{One Order}} \times \frac{\text{Demand per}}{\text{Period}}}{\text{Cost to Hold One Unit for One Period}}}$$

All orders are the same size. When the policy is implemented, demand per period is only one-half what was expected when order size was computed.
Consequently, actual total inventory cost will be _____ than if the expected demand per period had occurred and _____ than if the actual demand per period had been used to calculate order size.

A. larger; larger
B. larger; smaller
C. smaller; larger
D. smaller; smaller

13. Boyle Company has two decentralized divisions, X and Y. Division X has always purchased certain units from Division Y at $75 per unit. Because Division Y plans to raise the price to $100 per unit, Division X desires to purchase these units from outside suppliers for $75 per unit. Division Y's costs follow: 13.___

Y's variable costs per unit	$70
Y's annual fixed costs	$15,000
Y's annual production of these units for X	1,000 units

If Division X buys from an outside supplier, the facilities Division Y uses to manufacture these units would remain idle.
What would be the result if Boyle enforces a transfer price of $100 per unit between Divisions X and Y?
It would

A. be suboptimization for the company because X should buy from outside suppliers at $75 per unit
B. provide lower overall company net income than a transfer price of $75 per unit
C. provide higher overall company net income than a transfer price of $75 per unit
D. be more profitable for the company than allowing X to buy from outside suppliers at $75 per unit

Questions 14-16.

DIRECTIONS: Questions 14 through 16 are to be answered on the basis of the following information.

Shanley Corporation issued $2,000,000 of 6%, ten-year convertible bonds on June 1, 2005, at 98 plus accrued interest. The bonds were dated April 1, 2005, with interest payable April 1 and October 1. Bond discount is amortized semi-annually on a straight-line basis.

On April 1, 2006, $500,000 of these bonds were converted into 500 shares of $20 par value common stock. Accrued interest was paid in cash at the time of conversion.

14. If *accrued interest payable* were credited when the bonds were issued, what should be the amount of the debit to *interest expense* on October 1, 2006? 14.___
   A. Approximately $38,644 B. Exactly $40,000
   C. Approximately $41,356 D. Exactly $60,000

15. What should be the amount of the unamortized bond discount on April 1, 2006 relating to the bonds converted? 15.___
   A. Approximately $8,983 B. Approximately $9,153
   C. Exactly $10,000 D. Approximately $11,017

16. What was the effective interest rate on the bonds when they were issued? 16.___
   A. 6%
   B. Above 6%
   C. Below 6%
   D. Cannot be determined from the information given

17. What term identifies an accounting system in which the operations of the business are broken down into cost centers and the control function of a foreman, sales manager, or supervisor is emphasized? 17.___
   ______ accounting.
   A. Responsibility B. Operations-research
   C. Control D. Budgetary

18. Which of the following capital-expenditure planning and control techniques has been criticized because it fails to consider investment profitability? 18.___
   ______ method.
   A. Payback
   B. Average-return-on-investment
   C. Present-value
   D. Time-adjusted-rate-of-return

19. Which of the following capital-expenditure planning and control techniques has been criticized because it might mistakenly imply that earnings are reinvested at the rate of return earned by the investment? 19.___

______ method.
A. Payback
B. Average-return-on-investment
C. Present-value
D. Time-adjusted-rate-of-return

20. When a manufacturing company has a highly automated manufacturing plant producing many different products, what is probably the MOST appropriate basis of applying factory-overhead costs to work in process? 20.___
A. Direct-labor hours B. Direct-labor dollars
C. Machine hours D. Cost of materials used

KEY (CORRECT ANSWERS)

1.	B	11.	D
2.	C	12.	C
3.	A	13.	D
4.	B	14.	C
5.	B	15.	B
6.	C	16.	B
7.	D	17.	A
8.	C	18.	A
9.	A	19.	D
10.	D	20.	C

EXAMINATION SECTION

TEST 1

DIRECTIONS:
Each question or incomplete statement is followed by several suggested answers or completions. Select the one that *BEST* answers the question or completes the statement. *PRINT THE LETTER OF THE CORRECT ANSWER IN THE SPACE AT THE RIGHT.*

1. The use of a disclaimer of opinion might indicate that the auditor 1. ...
   A. is so uncertain with respect to an item that he cannot form an opinion on the fairness of presentation of the financial statements as a whole
   B. is uncertain with respect to an item that is material but not so material that he cannot form an opinion on the fairness of presentation of the financial statements as a whole
   C. has observed a violation of generally accepted accounting principles that has a material effect upon the fairness of presentation of financial statements, but is not so material that a qualified report is unjustified
   D. has observed a violation of generally accepted accounting principles that is so material that a qualified opinion is not justified
2. An auditor's "subject to" report is a type of 2. ...
   A. disclaimer of opinion B. qualified opinion
   C. adverse opinion D. standard opinion
3. An accountant will issue an adverse auditor's opinion if 3. ...
   A. the scope of his examination is limited by the client
   B. his exception to the fairness of presentation is so material that an "except for" opinion is not justified
   C. he did not perform sufficient auditing procedures to form an opinion on the financial statements taken as a whole
   D. such major uncertainties exist concerning the company's future that a "subject to" opinion is not justified
4. An auditor will express an "except for" opinion if 4. ...
   A. the client refuses to provide for a probable federal income tax deficiency that is material
   B. the degree of uncertainty associated with the client company's future makes a "subject to" opinion inappropriate
   C. he did not perform procedures sufficient to form an opinion on the consistency of application of generally accepted accounting principles
   D. he is basing his opinion in part upon work done by another auditor
5. Carl Sanborn, accountant, provides bookkeeping services to Alamo Products Co. He also is a director of Alamo and performs limited auditing procedures in connection with his preparation of Alamo's financial statements. Sanborn's report accompanying these financial statements should include a 5. ...
   A. detailed description of the limited auditing procedures performed

B. complete description of the relationships with Alamo that imperil Sanborn's independence
C. disclaimer of opinion and statement that financial statements are unaudited on each page of the financial statements
D. qualified opinion because of his lack of independence together with such assurance as his limited auditing procedures can provide

6. It was impracticable for an accountant to observe the physical inventory that his client conducted on the balance-sheet date. The accountant satisfied himself as to inventory quantities by other procedures. These procedures included making some physical counts of the inventory a week later and applying appropriate tests to intervening transactions. 6. ...
In his report on the financial statements, the accountant
A. must disclose the modification of the scope of his examination and express a qualified opinion
B. must disclose the modification of the scope of his examination, but may express an unqualified opinion
C. may omit reference to any modification of the scope of his examination and express an unqualified opinion
D. may omit reference to modification of the scope of his examination only if he describes the circumstances in an explanatory paragraph or his opinion paragraph

7. In connection with his examination of the financial statements of San Diego Co., an accountant is unable to form an opinion as to the proper statement of several accounts. A piecemeal opinion may be appropriate if 7. ...
A. the accounts in question are immaterial in terms of San Diego's financial position and results of operations
B. the failure to form an opinion is the result of restrictions imposed by the client
C. the piecemeal opinion is accompanied by a qualified opinion on the financial statements taken as a whole
D. in the auditor's judgment, the piecemeal opinion will serve a useful purpose

8. On its business stationery, an accounting firm should *NOT* list 8. ...
A. the firm's name, address, and telephone number
B. names of deceased partners in the firm name
C. membership in state accounting society
D. that it has tax expertise

9. An accountant should *reject* a management advisory services engagement if 9. ...
A. it would require him to make management decisions for an audit client
B. his recommendations are to be subject to review by the client
C. he audits the financial statements of a subsidiary of the prospective client
D. the proposed engagement is not accounting-related

10. When an accountant lacks independence in connection with an audit engagement, he should 10. ...
   A. state, in his auditor's report, the reason for his lack of independence
   B. disclaim an opinion on the financial statements
   C. list, in his auditor's report, all the generally accepted auditing procedures actually performed by him
   D. issue a piecemeal opinion

11. Tozzi, an accountant, has a small public accounting practice. One of Tozzi's clients desires services which Tozzi cannot adequately provide. Tozzi has recommended a larger firm, Casso & Co., to his client, and, in return, Casso has agreed to pay Tozzi 10% of the fee for services rendered by Casso for Tozzi's client. 11. ...
   Who, if anyone, is in violation of the AICPA's Code of Professional Ethics?
   A. *Both* Tozzi and Casso   B. *Neither* Tozzi nor Casso
   C. *Only* Tozzi   D. *Only* Casso

12. The accountant who regularly examines Venus Corporation's financial statements has been asked to prepare pro forma income statements for the next five years. If the statements are to be based upon the Corporation's operating assumptions and are for internal use only, the accountant should 12. ...
   A. *reject* the engagement because the statements are to be based upon assumptions
   B. *reject* the engagement because the statements are for internal use
   C. *accept* the engagement provided full disclosure is made of the assumptions used and the extent of the accountant's responsibility
   D. *accept* the engagement provided Venus certifies in writing that the statements are for internal use only

13. For purposes of expressing a piecemeal opinion, the threshold of materiality ordinarily is 13. ...
   A. *higher* (i.e., larger amounts are immaterial) because the auditor is not expressing an overall opinion on financial position and the results of operations
   B. *lower* (i.e., smaller amounts are material) because the individual items stand alone, thus affording a smaller base
   C. *unchanged* from the threshold that the auditor would use in expressing an overall opinion on financial position and the results of operations
   D. *not applicable* because piecemeal opinions may be used only for accounts that are subject to fairly exact quantification

14. In forming his opinion upon the consolidated financial statements of Saturn Corp., an accountant relies upon another auditor's examination of the financial statements of Io, Inc., a wholly owned subsidiary whose operations constitute 30% of Saturn's consolidated total. Io's auditor expresses an unqualified opinion on that company's financial statements. 14. ...

The accountant examining Saturn Corp. may be expected to express an unqualified opinion but refer to the report by the other auditor if he

A. concludes, based upon a review of the other auditor's professional standing and qualifications, that he is willing to assume the same responsibility as though he had performed the audit of Io's financial statements himself
B. is satisfied with the audit scope for the subsidiary, based upon his review of the audit program, but his inquiries disclose that the other auditor is not independent or lacks professional standing
C. is satisfied with the other auditor's professional standing but concludes, based upon a review of the audit program, that the audit scope for the examination of Io's financial statements was inadequate
D. is satisfied with the other auditor's professional reputation and audit scope but is unwilling to assume responsibility for the other auditor's work to the same extent as though he had performed the work himself

15. If a principal auditor decides that he will refer in his report to the examination of another auditor, he is required to disclose the 15. ...

A. name of the other auditor
B. nature of his inquiry into the other auditor's professional standing and extent of his review of the other auditor's work
C. portion of the financial statements examined by the other auditor
D. reasons why he is unwilling to assume responsibility for the other auditor's work

16. On August 15, 1985, an accountant completed field work on an examination of the financial statements of the Wyoming Corporation for the year ended June 30, 1985. On September 1, 1985, before issuance of the accountant's report on the financial statements, an event occurred that the accountant and Wyoming agree should be incorporated by footnote in the financial statements for the year ended June 30, 1985. The accountant has not otherwise reviewed events subsequent to the completion of field work. 16. ...

The accountant's report should be dated

A. September 1
B. June 30, except for the footnote, which should be dated September 1
C. August 15
D. August 15, except for the footnote, which should be dated September 1

17. In performing a review of his client's cash disbursements, an accountant uses systematic sampling with a random start. 17. ...

The *PRIMARY* disadvantage of systematic sampling is that population items

A. must be reordered in a systematic pattern before the sample can be drawn
B. may occur in a systematic pattern, thus negating the randomness of the sample
C. may occur twice in the sample
D. must be replaced in the population after sampling to permit valid statistical inference

18. From prior experience, an accountant is aware of the fact that cash disbursements contain a few unusually large disbursements. 18. ...
In using statistical sampling, the accountant's *BEST* course of action is to
A. *eliminate* any unusually large disbursements which appear in the sample
B. *continue* to draw new samples until no unusually large disbursements appear in the sample
C. *stratify* the cash-disbrusements population so that the unusually large disbursements are reviewed separately
D. *increase* the sample size to lessen the effect of the unusually large disbursements

19. In connection with his test of the accuracy of inventory counts, an accountant decides to use discovery sampling. Discovery sampling may be considered a special case of 19. ...
A. judgmental sampling B. sampling for variables
C. stratified sampling D. sampling for attributes

20. An accountant's test of the accuracy of inventory counts involves two storehouses. Storehouse A contains 10,000 inventory items and Storehouse B contains 5,000 items. The accountant plans to use sampling without replacement to test for an estimated 5% error rate. 20. ...
If the accountant's sampling plan calls for a specified reliability of 95% and a maximum tolerable error occurrence rate of 7.5% for both storehouses, the ratio of the size of the accountant's sample from Storehouse A to the size of the sample from Storehouse B should be
A. more than 1:1 but less than 2:1
B. 2:1 C. 1:1
D. more than .5:1 but less than 1:1

KEY (CORRECT ANSWERS)

1. A
2. B
3. B
4. A
5. C

6. C
7. D
8. D
9. A
10. B

11. B
12. C
13. B
14. D
15. C

16. D
17. B
18. C
19. D
20. A

TEST 2

DIRECTIONS:
Each question or incomplete statement is followed by several suggested answers or completions. Select the one that *BEST* answers the question or completes the statement. *PRINT THE LETTER OF THE CORRECT ANSWER IN THE SPACE AT THE RIGHT.*

1. Approximately 5% of the 10,000 homogeneous items included in Barrow's finished-goods inventory are believed to be defective. The accountant examining Barrow's financial statements decides to test this estimated 5% defective rate. He learns that, by sampling without replacement, a sample of 284 items from the inventory will permit specified reliability (confidence level) of 95% and specified precision (confidence interval) of ± .025. 1. ...
   If specified precision is changed to ± .05, and specified reliability remains 95%, the required sample size is
   A. 72 B. 335 C. 436 D. 1,543
2. The "reliability" (confidence level) of an estimate made from sample data is a mathematically determined figure that expresses the expected proportion of possible samples of a specified size from a given population 2. ...
   A. that will yield an interval estimate that will encompass the true population value
   B. that will yield an interval estimate that will not encompass the true population value
   C. for which the sample value and the population value are identical
   D. for which the sample elements will not exceed the population elements by more than a stated amount
3. In an examination of financial statements, an accountant generally will find stratified-sampling techniques to be *LEAST* appropriate to 3. ...
   A. examining charges to the maintenance account during the audit year
   B. tests of transactions for compliance with internal control
   C. the recomputation of a sample of factory-workers' net pay
   D. year-end confirmation of bank balances
4. An accountant's client wishes to determine inventory shrinkage by weighing a sample of inventory items. If a stratified random sample is to be drawn, the strata should be identified in such a way that 4. ...
   A. the overall population is divided into subpopulations of equal size so that each subpopulation can be given equal weight when estimates are made
   B. each stratum differs as much as possible with respect to expected shrinkage but the shrinkages expected for items within each stratum are as close as possible
   C. the sample mean and standard deviation of each individual stratum will be equal to the means and standard deviations of all other strata

D. the items in each stratum will follow a normal distribution so that probability theory can be used in making inferences from the sample data

5. In estimating the total value of supplies on repair trucks, Breaker Company draws random samples from two equal-sized strata of trucks. The mean value of the inventory stored on the larger trucks (stratum 1) was computed at $1,500, with a standard deviation of $250. On the smaller trucks (stratum 2), the mean value of inventory was computed as $500, with a standard deviation of $45.
If Breaker had drawn an unstratified sample from the entire population of trucks, the expected mean value of inventory per truck would be $1,000, and the expected standard deviation would be 5. ...
   A. *exactly* $147.50 B. *greater* than $250
   C. *less* than $45
   D. *between* $45 and $250, but not $147.50

6. An accountant conducting his first examination of the financial statements of Goldfang Corporation, is considering the propriety of reducing his work by consulting with the predecessor auditor and reviewing the predecessor's working papers.
This procedure is 6. ...
   A. acceptable
   B. required if the new auditor is to render an unqualified opinion
   C. acceptable only if the accountant refers in his report to his reliance upon the predecessor auditor's work
   D. unacceptable because the accountant should bring an independent viewpoint to a new engagement

7. The statement that *BEST* expresses the auditor's responsibility with respect to events occurring between the balance-sheet date and the end of his examination is that the 7. ...
   A. auditor has no responsibility for events occurring in the subsequent period unless these events affect transactions recorded on or before the balance-sheet date
   B. auditor's responsibility is to determine that a proper cutoff has been made and that transactions recorded on or before the balance-sheet date actually occurred
   C. auditor is fully responsible for events occurring in the subsequent period and should extend all detailed procedures through the last day of field work
   D. auditor is responsible for determining that a proper cutoff has been made and performing a general review of events occurring in the subsequent period

8. An auditor's unqualified short-form report 8. ...
   A. *implies* only that items disclosed in the financial statements and footnotes are properly presented and takes no position on the adequacy of disclosure

B. *implies* that disclosure is adequate in the financial statements and footnotes
C. *explicitly* states that disclosure is adequate in the financial statements and footnotes
D. *explicitly* states that all material items have been disclosed in conformity with generally accepted accounting principles

9. An accountant is completing his examination of the financial statements of the Jupiter Service Company for the year ended April 30, 1985. During the year, Jupiter's employees were granted an additional week's vacation, and this had a material effect upon vacation pay expense for the year and the accrued liability for vacation-pay at April 30, 1985. In the opinion of the accountant, this occurrence and its effects have been adequately disclosed in a footnote to the financial statements. In his auditor's report, the accountant *normally* will: 9. ...
A. Omit any mention of this occurrence and its effects
B. Refer to the footnote in his opinion paragraph but express an unqualified opinion
C. Refer to the footnote and express an opinion that is qualified as to consistency
D. Insist that comparative income statements for prior years be restated or express an opinion that is qualified as to consistency

10. While assisting Tension Co. in the preparation of unaudited financial statements, Walter Lamb, accountant, noted that Tension had increased property, plant, and equipment to reflect a recent property appraisal. In this circumstance, Mr. Lamb's reporting responsibility is met by 10. ...
A. issuing the statements on plain paper without reference to the accountant
B. advising Tension's management of the deviation from generally accepted accounting principles
C. describing the deviation from generally accepted accounting principles in his disclaimer of opinion
D. stating in his disclaimer of opinion that Tension's financial statements are unaudited

11. The *PRIMARY* responsibility for the adequacy of disclosure in the financial statements and footnotes rests with the 11. ...
A. partner assigned to the engagement
B. auditor in charge of field work
C. staffman who drafts the statements and footnotes
D. client

12. The use of an adverse opinion *generally* indicates: 12. ...
A. *Uncertainty* with respect to an item that is so material that the auditor cannot form an opinion on the fairness of presentation of the financial statements as a whole
B. *Uncertainty* with respect to an item that is material but not so material that the auditor cannot form an opinion on the fairness of the financial statements as a whole

C. *A violation* of generally accepted accounting principles that has a material effect upon the fairness of presentation of the financial statements, but is not so material that a qualified opinion is unjustified

D. *A violation* of generally accepted accounting principles that is so material that a qualified opinion is not justified

13. Purdue Sales Company asked an accountant's assistance in planning the use of multiple regression analysis to predict district sales. An equation has been estimated based upon historical data, and a standard error has been computed. 13. ...

When regression analysis based upon past periods is used to predict for a future period, the standard error associated with the predicted value, in relation to the standard error for the base equation, will be

A. smaller B. larger C. the same
D. larger or smaller, depending upon the circumstances

14. An accountant's client maintains perpetual inventory records. In the past, all inventory items have been counted on a cycle basis at least once during the year. Physical count and perpetual record differences have been minor. Now, the client wishes to minimize the cost of physically counting the inventory by changing to a sampling method in which many inventory items will not be counted during a given year. 14. ...

For purposes of expressing an opinion on his client's financial statements, the accountant will accept the sampling method *only* if

A. the sampling method has statistical validity
B. a stratified sampling plan is used
C. the client is willing to accept an opinion qualification in the auditor's report
D. the client is willing to accept a scope qualification in the auditor's report

15. Returns of positive-confirmation requests for accounts receivable were very poor. As an alternative procedure, the auditor decided to check subsequent collections. The auditor had satisfied himself that the client satisfactorily listed the customer name next to each check listed on the deposit slip; hence, he decided that ,for each customer for which a confirmation was not received, he would add all amounts shown for that customer on each validated deposit slip for the two months following the balance-sheet date. 15. ...

The *MAJOR* fallacy in the auditor's procedure is that

A. checking of subsequent collections is not an accepted alternative auditing procedure for confirmation of accounts receivable
B. by looking only at the deposit slip, the auditor would not know whether the payment was for the receivable at the balance-sheet data or a subsequent transaction

C. the deposit slip would not be received directly by the auditor as a confirmation would be
D. a customer may not have made a payment during the two-month period

16. Cherry Company, whose financial statements are unaudited, has engaged an accountant to make a special review and report on Cherry's internal accounting control. In general, to which of the following will this report be *LEAST* useful? 16. ...
A. Cherry's management
B. Present and prospective customers
C. A regulatory agency having jurisdiction over Cherry
D. The independent auditor of Cherry's parent company

17. Lapping would *MOST* likely be detected by 17. ...
A. examination of canceled checks clearing in the bank-cutoff period
B. confirming year-end bank balances
C. preparing a schedule of interbank transfers
D. investigating responses to account-receivable confirmations

18. From the standpoint of good procedural control, distributing payroll checks to employees is *BEST* handled by the 18. ...
A. accounting department B. personnel department
C. treasurer's department
D. employee's departmental supervisor

19. In a company whose materials and supplies include a great number of items, a *fundamental* deficiency in control requirements would be indicated if 19. ...
A. perpetual inventory records were not maintained for items of small value
B. the storekeeping function were to be combined with production and record-keeping
C. the cycle basis for physical inventory taking were to be used
D. minor supply items were to be expensed when purchased

20. In violation of company policy, the Monroe City Company erroneously capitalized the cost of painting its warehouse. The accountant examining Monroe City's financial statements *MOST* likely would learn of this by 20. ...
A. *reviewing* the listing of construction work orders for the year
B. *discussing* capitalization policies with the company controller
C. *observing*, during his physical inventory observation, that the warehouse had been painted
D. *examining* in detail a sample of construction work orders

KEY (CORRECT ANSWERS)

1. A	6. A	11. D	16. B
2. A	7. D	12. D	17. D
3. D	8. B	13. B	18. C
4. B	9. A	14. A	19. B
5. B	10. C	15. B	20. A

EXAMINATION SECTION
TEST 1

DIRECTIONS: Each question or incomplete statement is followed by several suggested answers or completions. Select the one that BEST answers the question or completes the statement. *PRINT THE LETTER OF THE CORRECT ANSWER IN THE SPACE AT THE RIGHT.*

1. Which of the following is NOT usually performed by the accountant in a review engagement of a nonpublic entity? 1.____

   A. Writing an engagement letter to establish an understanding regarding the services to be performed.
   B. Issuing a report stating that the review was performed in accordance with standards established by the AICPA.
   C. Communicating any material weaknesses discovered during the study and evaluation of internal accounting control.
   D. Reading the financial statements to consider whether they conform with generally accepted accounting principles.

2. When the financial statements are prepared on the going concern basis but the auditor concludes there is substantial doubt whether the client can continue in existence and also believes there are uncertainties about the recoverability of recorded asset amounts on the financial statements, the auditor may issue a(n) 2.____

   A. adverse opinion
   B. *except for* qualified opinion
   C. *subject to* qualified opinion
   D. unqualified opinion with an explanatory separate paragraph

3. A small client recently put its cash disbursements system on a microcomputer. About which of the following internal accounting control features would an auditor MOST likely be concerned? 3.____

   A. Programming of this microcomputer is in BASIC, although COBOL is the dominant, standard language for business processing.
   B. This microcomputer is operated by employees who have other, non-data-processing job responsibilities.
   C. The microcomputer terminal is physically close to the computer and directly connected to it.
   D. There are restrictions on the amount of data that can be stored and on the length of time that data can be stored.

4. When an independent accountant issues a comfort letter to an underwriter containing comments on data that have not been audited, the underwriter MOST likely will receive 4.____

   A. a disclaimer on prospective financial statements
   B. a limited opinion on *pro forma* financial statements
   C. positive assurance on supplementary disclosures
   D. negative assurance on capsule information

5. When an auditor conducts an examination in accordance with generally accepted auditing standards and concludes that the financial statements are fairly presented in accordance with a comprehensive basis of accounting other than generally accepted accounting principles such as the cash basis of accounting, the auditor should issue a 5.___

A. disclaimer of opinion
B. review report
C. qualified opinion
D. special report

6. A limitation on the scope of the auditor's examination sufficient to preclude an unqualified opinion will ALWAYS result when management 6.___

A. asks the auditor to report on the balance sheet and not on the other basic financial statements
B. refuses to permit its lawyer to respond to the letter of audit inquiry
C. discloses material related party transactions in the footnotes to the financial statements
D. knows that confirmation of accounts receivable is not feasible

7. Which of the following audit procedures would an auditor be LEAST likely to perform using a generalized computer audit program? 7.___

A. Searching records of accounts receivable balances for credit balances
B. Investigating inventory balances for possible obsolescence
C. Selecting accounts receivable for positive and negative confirmation
D. Listing of unusually large inventory balances

8. An auditor evaluates the existing system of internal accounting control PRIMARILY to 8.___

A. ascertain whether employees adhere to managerial policies
B. determine the extent of substantive tests that must be performed
C. determine whether procedures and records concerning the safeguarding of assets are reliable
D. establish a basis for deciding which compliance tests are necessary

9. When an independent CPA is associated with the financial statements of a publicly held entity but has not audited or reviewed such statements, the appropriate form of report to be issued must include a(n) 9.___

A. disclaimer of opinion
B. compilation report
C. adverse opinion
D. unaudited association report

10. An auditor includes a separate paragraph in an otherwise unqualified report to emphasize that the entity being reported upon had significant transactions with related parties. The inclusion of this separate paragraph 10.___

A. violates generally accepted auditing standards if this information is already disclosed in footnotes to the financial statements
B. necessitates a revision of the opinion paragraph to include the phrase *with the foregoing explanation*
C. is appropriate and would not negate the unqualified opinion
D. is considered an *except for* qualification of the report

11. Which of the following requires recognition in the auditor's opinion as to consistency? 11.____

    A. The correction of an error in the prior year's financial statements resulting from a mathematical mistake in capitalizing interest
    B. The change from the cost method to the equity method of accounting for investments in common stock
    C. A change in the estimate of provisions for warranty costs
    D. A change in depreciation method which has no effect on current year's financial statements but is certain to affect future years

12. The auditor who intends to express a qualified opinion should disclose all the substantive reasons in a separate explanatory paragraph of the report EXCEPT when the opinion paragraph 12.____

    A. makes reference to a contingent liability
    B. describes a limitation on the scope of the examination
    C. describes the use of an accounting principle at variance with generally accepted accounting principles
    D. makes reference to a change in accounting principle

13. When an examination is made in accordance with generally accepted auditing standards, the auditor should ALWAYS 13.____

    A. document the auditor's understanding of the client's internal accounting control system
    B. employ analytical review procedures
    C. obtain certain written representations from management
    D. observe the taking of physical inventory on the balance sheet date

14. Which of the following flowchart symbols represents online storage? 14.____

    A.

    B.
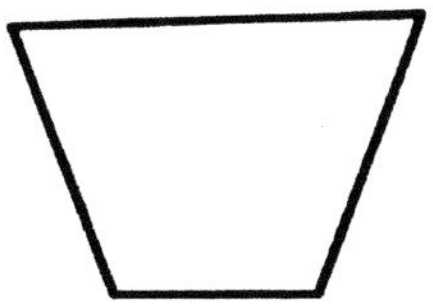

    C.
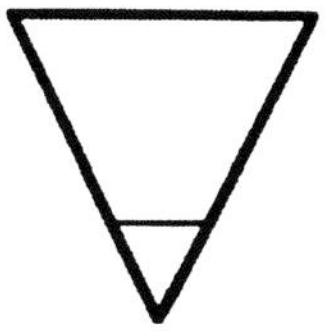

    D.
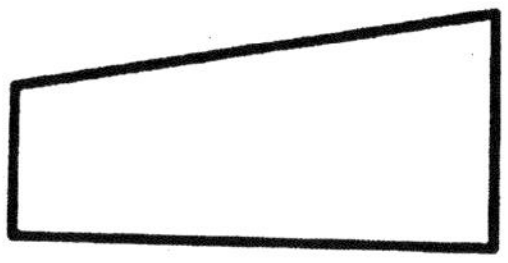

15. What is the continuing auditor's obligation concerning the discovery at an interim date of a material weakness in the internal accounting control of a client if this same weakness had been communicated to the client during the prior year's audit? 15.____
The auditor

    A. should communicate this weakness to the client immediately because the discovery of such weaknesses in internal accounting control is the purpose of a review of interim financial information
    B. need not communicate this weakness to the client because it had already been communicated the prior year

C. should communicate this weakness to the client following completion of the examination unless the auditor decides to communicate it to the client at the interim date
D. should extend the audit procedures to investigate whether this weakness had any effect on the prior year's financial statements

16. To achieve good internal accounting control, which department should perform the activities of matching shipping documents with sales orders and preparing daily sales summaries? 16.___

A. Billing
B. Shipping
C. Credit
D. Sales order

17. A PRIMARY advantage of using generalized audit software packages in auditing the financial statements of a client that uses an EDP system is that the auditor may 17.___

A. substantiate the accuracy of data through self-checking digits and hash totals
B. access information stored on computer files without a complete understanding of the client's hardware and software features
C. reduce the level of required compliance testing to a relatively small amount
D. gather and permanently store large quantities of supportive evidential matter in machine readable form

18. An auditor is concerned with completing various phases of the examination after the balance sheet date. 18.___
This subsequent period extends to the date of the

A. auditor's report
B. final review of the audit working papers
C. public issuance of the financial statements
D. delivery of the auditor's report to the client

19. The permanent file section of the working papers that is kept for each audit client MOST likely contains 19.___

A. review notes pertaining to questions and comments regarding the audit work performed
B. a schedule of time spent on the engagement by each individual auditor
C. correspondence with the client's legal counsel concerning pending litigation
D. narrative descriptions of the client's accounting procedures and internal accounting controls

20. If, after completing the review of the design of internal accounting controls, the auditor plans to rely on internal accounting control procedures pertaining to plant asset transactions, the auditor should NEXT 20.___

A. make extensive substantive tests of plant asset balances
B. establish the physical existence of current year additions
C. complete the plant asset section of the internal accounting control questionnaire
D. perform compliance tests of the controls expected to be relied upon

21. Sound internal accounting control procedures dictate that defective merchandise returned by customers should be presented to the ______ clerk. 21.____

A. purchasing
B. receiving
C. inventory control
D. sales

22. In a properly designed accounts payable system, a voucher is prepared after the invoice, purchase order, requisition, and receiving report are verified. 22.____
The NEXT step in the system is to

A. cancel the supporting documents
B. enter the check amount in the check register
C. approve the voucher for payment
D. post the voucher amount to the expense ledger

23. Alpha Company uses its sales invoices for posting perpetual inventory records. Inadequate internal accounting controls over the invoicing function allow goods to be shipped that are not invoiced. 23.____
The inadequate controls could cause an

A. understatement of revenues, receivables, and inventory
B. overstatement of revenues and receivables, and an understatement of inventory
C. understatement of revenues and receivables, and an overstatement of inventory
D. overstatement of revenues, receivables, and inventory

24. After an auditor had been engaged to perform the first audit for a nonpublic entity, the client requested to change the engagement to a review. 24.____
In which of the following situations would there be a reasonable basis to comply with the client's request?

A. The client's bank required an audit before committing to a loan, but the client subsequently acquired alternative financing.
B. The auditor was prohibited by the client from corresponding with the client's legal counsel.
C. Management refused to sign the client representation letter.
D. The auditing procedures were substantially complete and the auditor determined that an unqualified opinion was warranted, but there was a disagreement concerning the audit fee.

25. Which of the following statements BEST describe the auditor's responsibility regarding the detection of material irregularities? 25.____

A. Because of the inherent limitations of an audit, the auditor is not responsible for the failure to detect material irregularities.
B. The auditor is responsible for the failure to detect material irregularities when such failure results from nonperformance of audit procedures specifically described in the engagement letter.
C. The auditor should extend auditing procedures to actively search for evidence of material irregularities where the examination indicates that material irregularities may exist.
D. The auditor is responsible for the failure to detect material irregularities when the auditor's evaluation of internal accounting control indicates that there is no basis for any reliance thereon.

26. Comparative financial statements include the financial statements of a prior period which were examined by a predecessor auditor whose report is not presented. If the predecessor auditor's report was qualified, the successor auditor MUST 26.___

A. obtain written approval from the predecessor auditor to include the prior year's financial statements
B. issue a standard comparative audit report indicating the division of responsibility
C. express an opinion on the current year statements alone and make no reference to the prior year statements
D. disclose the reasons for any qualification in the predecessor auditor's opinion

27. The auditor may conclude that depreciation charges are insufficient by noting 27.___

A. large amounts of fully depreciated assets
B. continuous trade-ins of relatively new assets
C. excessive recurring losses on assets retired
D. insured values greatly in excess of book values

28. An auditor compares yearly revenues and expenses with those of the prior year and investigates all changes exceeding 10%. By this procedure, the auditor would be MOST likely to learn that 28.___

A. fourth quarter payroll taxes were not paid
B. the client changed its capitalization policy for small tools for the year
C. an increase in property tax rates has not been recognized in the client's accrual
D. the yearly provision for uncollectible accounts is inadequate because of worsening economic conditions

29. The development of constructive suggestions to clients for improvements in internal accounting control is 29.___

A. a requirement of the auditor's study and evaluation of internal accounting control
B. a desirable by-product of an audit engagement
C. addressed by the auditor only during a special engagement
D. as important as establishing a basis for reliance upon the internal accounting control system

30. Of the following statements about an internal accounting control system, which one is CORRECT? 30.___

A. The maintenance of the system of internal accounting control is an important responsibility of the internal auditor.
B. Administrative controls relate directly to the safeguarding of assets and the systems of authorization and approval.
C. Because of the cost/benefit relationship, internal accounting control procedures may be applied on a test basis in some circumstances.
D. Internal accounting control procedures reasonably ensure that collusion among employees cannot occur.

KEY (CORRECT ANSWERS)

1. C
2. C
3. B
4. D
5. D

6. B
7. B
8. B
9. A
10. C

11. B
12. D
13. C
14. A
15. C

16. A
17. B
18. A
19. D
20. D

21. B
22. C
23. C
24. A
25. C

26. D
27. C
28. B
29. B
30. C

TEST 2

DIRECTIONS: Each question or incomplete statement is followed by several suggested answers or completions. Select the one that BEST answers the question or completes the statement. *PRINT THE LETTER OF THE CORRECT ANSWER IN THE SPACE AT THE RIGHT.*

1. Which of the following statistical sampling methods is MOST useful to auditors when testing for compliance? 1.___

   A. Ratio estimation
   B. Variable sampling
   C. Difference estimation
   D. Discovery sampling

2. If after completing the preliminary phase of the review of the internal accounting control system the auditor plans to rely on the system, the auditor should NEXT 2.___

   A. trace several transactions through the related documents and records to observe the related internal accounting control procedures in operation
   B. perform compliance tests to provide reasonable assurance that the accounting control procedures are being applied as prescribed
   C. complete the review of the system to determine whether the accounting control procedures are suitably designed
   D. design substantive tests that contemplate reliance on the system of internal accounting control

3. The form of communication with a client in a management advisory service consultation should be 3.___

   A. either oral or written
   B. oral with appropriate documentation in the workpapers
   C. written and copies should be sent to both management and the board of directors
   D. written and a copy should be sent to management alone

4. Which of the following control procedures may prevent the failure to bill customers for some shipments? 4.___

   A. Each shipment should be supported by a prenumbered sales invoice that is accounted for.
   B. Each sales order should be approved by authorized personnel.
   C. Sales journal entries should be reconciled to daily sales summaries.
   D. Each sales invoice should be supported by a shipping document.

5. A part of the auditor's planning of an audit engagement should be a plan to search for 5.___

   A. errors or irregularities that would have a material or immaterial effect on the financial statements
   B. errors or irregularities that would have a material effect on the financial statements
   C. errors that would have a material effect on the financial statements, but the auditor need not plan to search for irregularities
   D. irregularities that would have a material effect on the financial statements, but the auditor need not plan to search for errors

6. In a study and evaluation of the system of internal accounting control, the completion of a questionnaire is MOST closely associated with which of the following? 6.____

   A. Tests of compliance
   B. Substantive tests
   C. Preliminary evaluation of the system
   D. Review of the system design

7. The audit work performed by each assistant should be reviewed to determine whether it was adequately performed and to evaluate whether 7.____

   A. there has been a thorough documentation of the internal accounting controls
   B. the auditor's system of quality control has been maintained at a high level
   C. the assistants' preliminary judgments about materiality differ from the materiality levels of the persons who will rely on the financial statements
   D. the results are consistent with the conclusions to be presented in the auditor's report

8. During a review of the financial statements of a nonpublic entity, the CPA finds that the financial statements contain a material departure from generally accepted accounting principles. 8.____
If management refuses to correct the financial statement presentations, the CPA should

   A. attach a footnote explaining the effects of the departure
   B. disclose the departure in a separate paragraph of the report
   C. issue a compilation report
   D. issue an adverse opinion

9. The profession's ethical standards would MOST likely be considered to have been violated when the CPA represents that specific consulting services will be performed for a stated fee and it is apparent at the time of the representation that the 9.____

   A. CPA would not be independent
   B. fee was a competitive bid
   C. actual fee would be substantially higher
   D. actual fee would be substantially lower than the fees charged by other CPAs for comparable services

10. After the preliminary phase of the review of a client's EDP controls, an auditor may decide not to perform compliance tests related to the control procedures within the EDP portion of the client's internal accounting control system. 10.____
Which of the following would NOT be a valid reason for choosing to omit compliance tests?

   A. The controls appear adequate.
   B. The controls duplicate operative controls existing elsewhere in the system.
   C. There appear to be major weaknesses that would preclude reliance on the stated procedure.
   D. The time and dollar costs of testing exceed the time and dollar savings in substantive testing if the compliance tests show the controls to be operative.

11. Before applying principal substantive tests to the details of asset and liability accounts at an interim date, the auditor should 11.___

A. assess the difficulty in controlling incremental audit risk
B. investigate significant fluctuations that have occurred in the asset and liability accounts since the previous balance sheet date
C. select only those accounts which can effectively be sampled during year-end audit work
D. consider the compliance tests that must be applied at the balance sheet date to extend the audit conclusions reached at the interim date

12. A violation of the profession's ethical standards would MOST likely occur when a CPA who 12.___

A. is also admitted to the Bar represents on letterhead to be both an attorney and a CPA
B. writes a newsletter on financial management also permits a publishing company to solicit subscriptions by direct mail
C. is controller of a bank permits the bank to use the controller's CPA title in the listing of officers in its publications
D. is the sole shareholder in a professional accountancy corporation that uses the designation *and company* in the firm title

13. After beginning an audit of a new client, Larkin, CPA, discovers that the professional competence necessary for the engagement is lacking. Larkin informs management of the situation and recommends another CPA, and management engages the other CPA. Under these circumstances, 13.___

A. Larkin's lack of competence should be construed to be a violation of generally accepted auditing standards
B. Larkin may request compensation from the client for any professional services rendered to it in connection with the audit
C. Larkin's request for a commission from the other CPA is permitted because a more competent audit can now be performed
D. Larkin may be indebted to the other CPA since the other CPA can collect from the client only the amount the client originally agreed to pay Larkin

14. Which of the following BEST describes what is meant by generally accepted auditing standards? 14.___

A. Pronouncements issued by the Auditing Standards Board
B. Procedures to be used to gather evidence to support financial statements
C. Rules acknowledged by the accounting profession because of their universal compliance
D. Measures of the quality of the auditor's performance

15. A CPA purchased stock in a client corporation and placed it in a trust as an educational fund for the CPA's minor child. The trust securities were not material to the CPA but were material to the child's personal net worth. Would the independence of the CPA be considered to be impaired with respect to the client? 15.___

A. *Yes,* because the stock would be considered a direct financial interest and, consequently, materiality is not a factor

B. *Yes,* because the stock would be considered an indirect financial interest that is material to the CPA's child
C. *No,* because the CPA would not be considered to have a direct financial interest in the client
D. *No,* because the CPA would not be considered to have a material indirect financial interest in the client

16. The auditor concludes that there is a material inconsistency in the other information in an annual report to shareholders containing audited financial statements. 16._____
If the client refuses to revise or eliminate the material inconsistency, the auditor should

A. revise the auditor's report to include a separate explanatory paragraph describing the material inconsistency
B. consult with a party whose advice might influence the client, such as the client's legal counsel
C. issue a qualified opinion after discussing the matter with the client's board of directors
D. consider the matter closed since the other information is not in the audited financial statements

17. One of the major problems in an EDP system is that incompatible functions may be performed by the same individual. One compensating control for this is the use of 17._____

A. a self-checking digit system
B. echo checks
C. a computer log
D. computer-generated hash totals

18. An auditor plans to examine a sample of 20 purchase orders for proper approvals as prescribed by the client's internal accounting control procedures. One of the purchase orders in the chosen sample of 20 cannot be found, and the auditor is unable to use alternative procedures to test whether that purchase order was properly approved. The auditor should 18._____

A. choose another purchase order to replace the missing purchase order in the sample
B. consider this compliance test invalid and proceed with substantive tests since internal accounting control cannot be relied upon
C. treat the missing purchase order as a deviation for the purpose of evaluating the sample
D. select a completely new set of 20 purchase orders

19. Where computer processing is used in significant accounting applications, internal accounting control procedures may be defined by classifying control procedures into two types: general and 19._____

A. administrative
B. specific
C. application
D. authorization

20. The principal auditor is satisfied with the independence and professional reputation of the other auditor who has audited a subsidiary. 20.___
To indicate the division of responsibility, the principal auditor should modify

A. both the scope and opinion paragraphs of the report
B. only the scope paragraph of the report
C. only the opinion paragraph of the report
D. only the opinion paragraph of the report and include an explanatory middle paragraph

21. When the auditor is unable to determine the amounts associated with the illegal acts of client personnel because of an inability to obtain adequate evidence, the auditor should issue a(n) 21.___

A. *subject to* qualified opinion
B. disclaimer of opinion
C. adverse opinion
D. unqualified opinion with a separate explanatory paragraph

22. An auditor would be MOST likely to consider expressing a qualified opinion if the client's financial statements include a footnote on related party transactions that 22.___

A. lists the amounts due from related parties including the terms and manner of settlement
B. discloses compensating balance arrangements maintained for the benefit of related parties
C. represents that certain transactions with related parties were consummated on terms equally as favorable as would have been obtained in transactions with unrelated parties
D. presents the dollar volume of related party transactions and the effects of any change in the method of establishing terms from that of the prior period

23. After issuance of the auditor's report, the auditor has no obligation to make any further inquiries with respect to audited financial statements covered by that report unless 23.___

A. a final resolution of a contingency that had resulted in a qualification of the auditor's report is made
B. a development occurs that may affect the client's ability to continue as a going concern
C. an investigation of the auditor's practice by a peer review committee ensues
D. new information is discovered concerning undisclosed related party transactions of the previously audited period

24. The accountant's report expressing an opinion on an entity's system of internal accounting control would NOT include a 24.___

A. brief explanation of the broad objectives and inherent limitations of internal accounting control
B. specific date that the report covers, rather than a period of time
C. statement that the entity's system of internal accounting control is consistent with that of the prior year after giving effect to subsequent changes
D. description of the scope of the engagement

25. Which of the following legal situations would be considered to impair the auditor's independence? 25.____

A. An expressed intention by the present management to commence litigation against the auditor alleging deficiencies in audit work for the client, although the auditor considers that there is only a remote possibility that such a claim will be filed
B. Actual litigation by the auditor against the client for an amount not material to the auditor or to the financial statements of the client arising out of disputes as to billings for management advisory services
C. Actual litigation by the auditor against the present management alleging management fraud or deceit
D. Actual litigation by the client against the auditor for an amount not material to the auditor or to the financial statements of the client arising out of disputes as to billings for tax services

26. The PRIMARY reason an auditor requests letters of inquiry be sent to a client's attorneys is to provide the auditor with 26.____

A. a description and evaluation of litigation, claims, and assessments that existed at the date of the balance sheet
B. an expert opinion as to whether a loss is possible, probable, or remote
C. the opportunity to examine the documentation concerning litigation, claims, and assessments
D. corroboration of the information furnished by management concerning litigation, claims, and assessments

27. In connection with the element of professional development, a CPA firm's system of quality control should ordinarily provide that all personnel 27.____

A. have the knowledge required to enable them to fulfill responsibilities assigned
B. possess judgment, motivation, and adequate experience
C. seek assistance from persons having appropriate levels of knowledge, judgment, and authority
D. demonstrate compliance with peer review directives

28. Edwards Corp. uses the last-in, first-out method of costing for half of its inventory and the first-in, first-out method of costing for the other half of its inventory. 28.____
Because of these recording and reporting methods, the auditor should issue a(n) _______ opinion.

A. unqualified
B. disclaimer of
C. *except for* qualified
D. *subject to* qualified

29. Purchase cutoff procedures should be designed to test whether or not all inventory 29.____

A. purchased and received before the end of the year was paid for
B. ordered before the end of the year was received
C. purchased and received before the end of the year was recorded
D. owned by the company is in the possession of the company at the end of the year

30. Matthews Corp. has changed from a system of recording time worked on clock cards to a computerized payroll system in which employees record time in and out with magnetic cards. The EDP system automatically updates all payroll records. Because of this change, 30.___

A. a generalized computer audit program must be used
B. part of the audit trail is altered
C. the potential for payroll related fraud is diminished
D. transactions must be processed in batches

KEY (CORRECT ANSWERS)

1.	D	16.	A
2.	C	17.	C
3.	A	18.	C
4.	A	19.	C
5.	B	20.	A
6.	D	21.	B
7.	D	22.	C
8.	B	23.	D
9.	C	24.	C
10.	A	25.	C
11.	A	26.	D
12.	D	27.	A
13.	B	28.	A
14.	D	29.	C
15.	A	30.	B

EXAMINATION SECTION
TEST 1

DIRECTIONS: Each question or incomplete statement is followed by several suggested answers or completions. Select the one that *BEST* answers the question or completes the statement. *PRINT THE LETTER OF THE CORRECT ANSWER IN THE SPACE AT THE RIGHT.*

1. On April 14, 2009, an accountant issued an unqualified opinion on the financial statements of the Waldo Company for the year ended February 28, 2009. A structural defect in Waldo's recently completed plant first appeared in late 2008, but the accountant did not learn of it until April 25, 2009. On May 1, 2009, the accountant learned that the defect would cause material losses to the Company. The accountant's PRIMARY responsibility is 1._____

   A. to determine that immediate steps are taken to inform all parties who are relying on information contained in the statements
   B. to make certain that the company plans to provide for the losses in its financial statements for the year ended February 28, 2009
   C. to withdraw his unqualified opinion on the financial statements for the year ended February 28, 2009, and issue a disclaimer of opinion or an appropriately qualified opinion
   D. advisory only since the structural defect was not disclosed until after the completion of field work

2. In connection with a public offering of first mortgage bonds by Ronzoni Corp., the bond underwriter has asked Ronzoni's accountant to furnish him with a "comfort letter" giving as much assurance as possible relative to Ronzoni's unaudited financial statements for the three months ended March 31, 2009. The accountant had expressed an unqualified opinion on Ronzoni's financial statements for the year ended December 31, 2008; he has performed a limited review of Ronzoni's financial statements for the three months ended March 31, 2009. Nothing has come to his attention that would indicate that the March 31, 2009 statements are not properly presented. Under these circumstances, the accountant's response to the underwriter's request should be to 2._____

   A. give negative assurance as to the March 31, 2009 financial statements but disclaim an opinion on these statements
   B. inform the underwriters that no comfort letter is possible without an audit of the financial statements for the three months ended March 31, 2009
   C. furnish to the underwriters an opinion that the March 31, 2009 statements are fairly presented subject to year-end audit adjustments
   D. furnish to the underwriters a piecemeal opinion covering financial statements for the three months ended March 31, 2009

3. One of the generally accepted auditing standards specifies that the auditor 3._____

   A. inspect all fixed assets acquired during the year
   B. base his fees upon cost
   C. make a proper study and evaluation of the existing internal control
   D. may not solicit clients

4. An auditor's opinion exception arising from a limitation on the scope of his examination should be explained in 4._

A. a footnote to the financial statements
B. the auditor's report
C. both a footnote to the financial statements and the auditor's report
D. both the financial statements (immediately after the caption of the item or items which could not be verified) and the auditor's report

5. An auditor need make no reference in his report to limitations on the scope of his audit if he 5._

A. finds it impracticable to confirm receivables but satisfies himself by other procedures
B. does not audit the financial statements of an unaudited subsidiary that represents 75% of the parent's total assets
C. omits confirmation of receivables at the client's request but satisfies himself by other procedures
D. does not observe the opening inventory and is unable to satisfy himself by other procedures

6. An auditor's "except for" report is a type of 6._

A. adverse opinion
B. "subject to" opinion
C. qualified opinion
D. disclaimer of opinion

7. The opinion paragraph of an accountant's report begins: "In our opinion, based upon our examination and the report of other auditors, the accompanying consolidated balance sheet and consolidated statements of income and retained earnings and of changes in financial position present fairly ...." 7._
This is a(n)

A. partial disclaimer of opinion
B. unqualified opinion
C. "except for" opinion
D. qualified opinion

8. Even though he is expressing an unqualified opinion on the financial statements of Tigris Corporation, an accountant feels that readers of the financial statements should be aware of an unusual auditing procedure that he used. 8._
For this purpose, he should describe the procedure in the

A. general representation letter
B. opinion paragraph of his report
C. scope paragraph of his report
D. footnotes to the financial statements

9. Approximately 90% of Rubinstein's Holding Company's assets consist of investments in wholly owned subsidiary companies. The accountant examining Rubinstein's financial statements has satisfied himself that changes in underlying equity in these investments have been properly computed based upon the subsidiaries' unaudited financial statements, but he has not examined the subsidiaries' financial statements. 9._

The auditor's report should include a(n)

A. adverse opinion
B. "except for" opinion
C. "subject to" opinion
D. disclaimer of opinion

10. An accountant has been engaged to prepare unaudited financial statements for his client. 10.____
Which of the following statements BEST describes this engagement? The

A. accountant must perform the basic accepted auditing standards necessary to determine that the statements are in conformity with generally accepted accounting principles
B. accountant is performing an accounting service rather than an examination of the financial statements
C. financial statements are representations of both management and the accountant
D. accountant may prepare the statements from the books, but may not assist in adjusting and closing the books

11. The accountant's reporting responsibilities are NOT met by attaching an explanation of the circumstances and a disclaimer of opinion to financial statements if the accountant 11.____

A. has neither confirmed receivables nor observed the taking of the physical inventory
B. believes that the financial statements are false or misleading
C. is uncertain about the outcome of a material contingency
D. has not performed sufficient auditing procedures to express an opinion

12. Footnotes to financial statements should NOT be used to 12.____

A. describe the nature and effect of a change in accounting principles
B. identify substantial differences between book and tax income
C. correct an improper financial statement presentation
D. indicate bases for valuing assets

13. Assuming that none of the following has been disclosed in the financial statements, the MOST appropriate item for footnote disclosure is the 13.____

A. collection of all receivables subsequent to year-end
B. revision of employees' pension plan
C. retirement of president of company and election of new president
D. material decrease in the advertising budget for the coming year and its anticipated effect upon income

14. An exception in the auditor's report because of the lack of consistent application of generally accepted accounting principles MOST likely would be required in the event of 14.____

A. a change in the rate of provision for uncollectible accounts based upon collection experience
B. the original adoption of a pension plan for employees
C. inclusion of a previously unconsolidated subsidiary in consolidated financial statements
D. the revision of pension plan actuarial assumptions based upon experience

15. An accountant who believes the occurrence rate of a certain characteristic in a population being examined is 3% and who has established a maximum acceptable occurrence rate at 5%, should use a(n) _______ sampling plan. 15.___

A. attribute B. discovery C. stratified D. variable

16. For good internal control, the monthly bank statements should be reconciled by someone under the direction of the 16.___

A. credit manager
B. controller
C. cashier
D. treasurer

17. For good internal control, the person who should sign checks is the 17.___

A. person preparing the checks
B. purchasing agent
C. accounts-payable clerk
D. treasurer

18. For good internal control, the credit manager should be responsible to the 18.___

A. sales manager
B. customer-service manager
C. controller
D. treasurer

19. For good internal control, the billing department should be under the direction of the 19.___

A. controller
B. credit manager
C. sales manager
D. treasurer

20. The authorization for write-off of accounts receivable should be the responsibility of the 20.___

A. credit manager
B. controller
C. accounts-receivable clerk
D. treasurer

KEY (CORRECT ANSWERS)

1.	A	11.	B
2.	A	12.	C
3.	C	13.	B
4.	B	14.	C
5.	A	15.	A
6.	C	16.	B
7.	B	17.	D
8.	C	18.	D
9.	D	19.	A
10.	B	20.	D

TEST 2

DIRECTIONS: Each question or Incomplete statement is followed by several suggested answers or completions. Select the one that *BEST* answers the question or completes the statement. *PRINT THE LETTER OF THE CORRECT ANSWER IN THE SPACE AT THE RIGHT.*

1. Emerson, Inc., has a June 30 year-end. Its bank mails bank statements each Friday of every week and on the last business day of each month. 1.____
   For year-end, Saturday, June 30, the auditor should have the client ask the bank to mail directly to the auditor

   A. *only* the June 29 bank statement
   B. *only* the July 13 bank statement
   C. *both* the June 29 and July 6 bank statements
   D. *both* the July 6 and 13 bank statements

2. Uranus Company has a separate outside transfer agent and outside registrar for its common stock. 2.____
   A confirmation request sent to the transfer agent should ask for

   A. a list of all stockholders and the number of shares issued to each
   B. a statement from the agent that all surrendered certificates have been effectively canceled
   C. total shares issued, shares issued in name of client, and unbilled fees
   D. total shares authorized

3. The Miller Company records checks as being issued on the day they are written; however, the checks are often held a number of days before being released. 3.____
   The audit procedure which is LEAST likely to reveal this method of incorrect cash-disbursements cutoff is to

   A. examine checks returned with cutoff bank statement for unreasonable time lag between date recorded in cash-disbursements book and date clearing bank
   B. reconcile vendors' invoices with accounts payable per books
   C. reconcile bank statement at year-end
   D. reconcile exceptions to account-payable confirmations

4. The Sandman Corporation uses prenumbered receiving reports which are released in numerical order from a locked box. For two days before the physical count, all receiving reports are stamped "before inventory," and, for two days after the physical count, all receiving reports are stamped "after inventory." The receiving department continues to receive goods after the cutoff time while the physical count is in process. 4.____
   The LEAST efficient method for checking the accuracy of the cutoff is to

   A. list the number of the last receiving report for items included in the physical-inventory count
   B. observe that the receiving clerk is stamping the receiving reports properly
   C. test trace receiving reports issued before the last receiving report to the physical items to see that they have been included in the physical count
   D. test trace receiving reports issued after the last receiving report to the physical items to see that they have not been included in the physical count

5. Lustig & Co., accountants, are the auditors of Ledley Corporation which has a subsidiary audited by Tompkins & Co., accountants. Tompkins issued a qualified opinion on the financial statements of the subsidiary because of an uncertainly on the recovery of deferred-research-and-development costs. 5.___
Lustig can issue an unqualified opinion on the consolidated financial statements of Leslie and subsidiaries *only* if

A. the amount of the subsidiary's deferred-research-and-development costs is not material in relation to the consolidated statements
B. Lustig is able to satisfy itself as to the independence and professional reputation of Tompkins
C. Lustig is able to satisfy itself as to the independence and professional reputation of Tompkins and also take appropriate steps to satisfy itself as to the quality of Tompkin's examination
D. Lustig makes reference in its report to the examination of the subsidiary by Tompkins

6. Benn, Inc., carries its investment in Monania Corporation at equity. Benn's investment in Monania accounts for 45% of the total assets of Benn. Benn and Monania are not audited by the same accountant. 6.___
In order for Benn's auditor to issue an unqualified opinion in regard to the value of Benn's investment in Monania and the income derived therefrom, Benn's auditor

A. needs to obtain only Monania's unaudited financial statements
B. needs to obtain only Monania's audited financial statements
C. must obtain Monania's audited financial statements and make inquiries concerning the professional reputation and independence of Monania's auditor
D. must review the working papers of Monania's auditor

7. Devore, Inc., which has a December 31 year-end, closed an out-of-town division on April 21, 2008. The checking account used by the division at a local bank was closed out as of April 21, 2008. The bank, however, has continued to mail bank statements, with zero balances, as of the fifth of each month. Devore has requested the bank to mail the January 5, 2009 bank statement directly to its independent auditor. 7.___
For this closed checking account during his examination for 2008, the auditor should *ordinarily*

A. review *only* the January 5, 2009, bank statement
B. review *only* the bank statement for 2008
C. review *only* the bank statements for 2008 and the January 5, 2009, statement
D. send a bank confirmation as of December 31, 2008, in addition to reviewing the bank statements for 2008 and the January 5, 2009, statement

8. The audit step MOST likely to reveal the existence of contingent liabilities is: 8.___

A. A review of vouchers paid during the month following the year-end
B. Account-payable confirmations
C. An inquiry directed to legal counsel
D. Mortgage-note confirmation

9. One of the MAJOR audit procedures for determining whether the allowance for doubtful receivables is adequate is 9.____

A. the preparation of a list of aged accounts receivable
B. confirming any account receivable written off during the year
C. vouching the collection on any account receivable written off in prior periods
D. confirming any account receivable with a credit balance

10. One of the *better* ways for an auditor to detect kiting is to 10.____

A. request a cut-off bank statement
B. send a bank confirmation
C. prepare a bank-transfer working paper
D. prepare a bank reconciliation at year end

11. A company uses the account code 448 for maintenance expense. However, one of the company's clerks often codes maintenance expense as 844. The highest account code in the system is 800. 11.____
What would be the BEST internal control check to build into the company's computer program to detect this error?

A. A check for this type of error would have to be made before the information was transmitted to the EDP department
B. Valid-character test
C. Sequence check
D. Valid-code test

12. Parsons is the executive partner of Parsons & Co., accountants. One of its smaller clients is a large nonprofit charitable organization. The organization has asked Parsons to be on its board of directors which consists of a large number of the community's leaders. Membership on the board is honorary in nature. Parsons & Co. would be considered to be independent 12.____

A. under no circumstances
B. as long as Parsons' directorship was disclosed in the organization's financial statements
C. as long as Parsons was not directly in charge of the audit
D. as long as Parsons does not perform or give advice on management functions of the organization

13. Godley, a non-CPA, has a law practice. Godley has recommended one of his clients to Dawson, CPA. Dawson has agreed to pay Godley 10% of the fee for services rendered by Dawson to Godley's client. 13.____
Who, if anyone, is in violation of the Code of Professional Ethics?

A. *Both* Godley and Dawson
B. *Neither* Godley nor Dawson
C. *Only* Godette
D. *Only* Dawson

14. The general group of the generally accepted auditing standards includes a requirement that 14.____

A. the field work be adequately planned and supervised
B. the auditor's report state whether or not the financial statements conform to generally accepted accounting principles

C. due professional care be exercised by the auditor
D. informative disclosures in the financial statements be reasonably adequate

15. Approximately 95% of returned positive account-receivable confirmations indicated that the customer owed a smaller balance than the amount confirmed. 15.___
This might be explained by the fact that

A. the cash-receipts journal was held open after year-end
B. there is a large number of unrecorded liabilities
C. the sales journal was closed prior to year-end
D. the sales journal was held open after year-end

16. An auditor should examine minutes of board of directors' meetings 16.___

A. through the date of his report
B. through the date of the financial statements
C. on a test basis
D. only at the beginning of the audit

17. The return of a positive account-receivable confirmation without an exception attests to the 17.___

A. collectibility of the receivable balance
B. accuracy of the receivable balance
C. accuracy of the aging of accounts receivable
D. accuracy of the allowance for bad debts

18. During his examination of a January 19, 2009, cut-off bank statement, an auditor noticed that the majority of checks listed as outstanding at December 31, 2008 had not cleared the bank. This would indicate: 18.___

A. A high probability of lapping
B. A high probability of kiting
C. That the cash-disbursements journal had been held open past December 31, 2008
D. That the cash-disbursements journal had been closed prior to December 31, 2008

19. A PRINCIPAL purpose of a letter of representation from management is to 19.___

A. serve as an introduction to company personnel and an authorization to examine the records
B. discharge the auditor from legal liability for his examination
C. confirm in writing management's approval of limitations on the scope of the audit
D. remind management of its primary responsibility for financial statements

20. As the specified reliability is increased in a discovery sampling plan for any given population and maximum occurrence rate, the required sample size 20.___

A. increases
B. decreases
C. remains the same
D. cannot be determined

KEY (CORRECT ANSWERS)

1.	D	11.	D
2.	C	12.	D
3.	C	13.	D
4.	B	14.	C
5.	A	15.	D
6.	C	16.	A
7.	D	17.	B
8.	C	18.	C
9.	A	19.	D
10.	C	20.	A

EXAMINATION SECTION
TEST 1

DIRECTIONS: Each question or incomplete statement is followed by several suggested answers or completions. Select the one that BEST answers the question or completes the statement. *PRINT THE LETTER OF THE CORRECT ANSWER IN THE SPACE AT THE RIGHT.*

1. *Which one* of the following generalizations is *most likely* to be INACCURATE and lead to judgmental errors in communication? 1.____

   A. A supervisor must be able to read with understanding
   B. Misunderstanding may lead to dislike
   C. Anyone can listen to another person and understand what he means
   D. It is usually desirable to let a speaker talk until he is finished

2. Assume that, as a supervisor, you have been directed to inform your subordinates about the implementation of a new procedure which will affect their work. While communicating this information, you should do all of the following EXCEPT 2.____

   A. obtain the approval of your subordinates regarding the new procedure
   B. explain the reason for implementing the new procedure
   C. hold a staff meeting at a time convenient to most of your subordinates
   D. encourage a productive discussion of the new procedure

3. Assume that you are in charge of a section that handles requests for information on matters received from the public. One day, you observe that a clerk under your supervision is using a method to log-in requests for information that is different from the one specified by you in the past. Upon questioning the clerk, you discover that instructions changing the old procedure were delivered orally by your supervisor on a day on which you were absent from the office. 3.____
   Of the following, the *most appropriate* action for you to take is to

   A. tell the clerk to revert to the old procedure at once
   B. ask your supervisor for information about the change
   C. call your staff together and tell them that no existing procedure is to be changed unless you direct that it be done
   D. write a memo to your supervisor suggesting that all future changes in procedure are to be in writing and that they be directed to you

4. At the first meeting with your staff after appointment as a supervisor, you find considerable indifference and some hostility among the participants. 4.____
   Of the following, the *most appropriate* way to handle this situation is to

   A. disregard the attitudes displayed and continue to make your presentation until you have completed it
   B. discontinue your presentation but continue the meeting and attempt to find out the reasons for their attitudes
   C. warm up your audience with some good natured statements and anecdotes and then proceed with your presentation
   D. discontinue the meeting and set up personal interviews with the staff members to try to find out the reason for their attitude

5. In order to start the training of a new employee, it has been a standard practice to have him read a manual of instructions or procedures. 5.___
This method is currently being replaced by the _________ method.

A. audio-visual
B. conference
C. lecture
D. programmed instruction

6. Of the following subjects, the *one* that can usually be *successfully* taught by a first-line supervisor who is training his subordinates is: 6.___

A. Theory and philosophy of management
B. Human relations
C. Responsibilities of a supervisor
D. Job skills

7. Assume that as a supervisor you are training a clerk who is experiencing difficulty learning a new task. 7.___
Which one of the following would be the LEAST effective approach to take when trying to solve this problem? To

A. ask questions which will reveal the clerk's understanding of the task
B. take a different approach in explaining the task
C. give the clerk an opportunity to ask questions about the task
D. make sure the clerk knows you are watching his work closely

8. One school of management and supervision involves participation by employees in the setting of group goals and in the sharing of responsibility for the operation of the unit. 8.___
If this philosophy were applied to a unit consisting of professional and clerical personnel, one should expect

A. the professional and clerical personnel to participate with equal effectiveness in operating areas and policy areas
B. the professional personnel to participate with greater effectiveness than the clerical personnel in policy areas
C. the clerical personnel to participate with greater effectiveness than the professional personnel in operating areas
D. greater participation by clerical personnel but with less responsibility for their actions

9. With regard to productivity, high morale among employees *generally* indicates a 9.___

A. history of high productivity
B. nearly absolute positive correlation with high productivity
C. predisposition to be productive under facilitating leadership and circumstances
D. complacency which has little effect on productivity

10. Assume that you are going to organize the professionals and clerks under your supervision into work groups or teams of two or three employees. 10.___
Of the following, the step which is LEAST likely to foster the successful development of each group is to

A. allow friends to work together in the group
B. provide special help and attention to employees with no friends in their group
C. frequently switch employees from group to group
D. rotate jobs within the group in order to strengthen group identification

11. Following are four statements which might be made by an employee to his supervisor during a performance evaluation interview. 11.____
Which of the statements BEST provides a basis for developing a plan to improve the employee's performance?

A. *I understand that you are dissatisfied with my work and I will try harder in the future.*
B. *I feel that I've been making too many careless clerical errors recently.*
C. *I am aware that I will be subject to disciplinary action if my work does not improve within one month.*
D. *I understand that this interview is simply a requirement of your job, and not a personal attack on me.*

12. Three months ago, Mr. Smith and his supervisor, Mrs. Jones, developed a plan which was intended to correct Mr. Smith's inadequate job performance. Now, during a follow-up interview, Mr. Smith, who thought his performance had satisfactorily improved, has been informed that Mrs. Jones is still dissatisfied with his work. 12.____
Of the following, it is *most likely* that the disagreement occurred because, when formulating the plan ,they did NOT

A. set realistic goals for Mr. Smith Is performance
B. set a reasonable time limit for Mr. Smith to effect his improvement in performance
C. provide for adequate training to improve Mr. Smith's skills
D. establish performance standards for measuring Mr. Smith's progress

13. When a supervisor delegates authority to subordinates, there are usually many problems to overcome, such as inadequately trained subordinates and poor planning. 13.____
All of the following are means of increasing the effectiveness of delegation EXCEPT:

A. Defining assignments in the light of results expected
B. Maintaining open lines of communication
C. Establishing tight controls so that subordinates will stay within the bounds of the area of delegation
D. Providing rewards for successful assumption of authority by a subordinate

14. Assume that one of your subordinates has arrived late for work several times during the current month. The last time he was late you had warned him that another unexcused lateness would result in formal disciplinary action. 14.____
If the employee arrives late for work again during this month, the FIRST action you should take is to

A. give the employee a chance to explain this lateness
B. give the employee a written copy of your warning
C. tell the employee that you are recommending formal disciplinary action
D. tell the employee that you will give him only one more chance before recommending formal disciplinary action

15. In trying to decide how many subordinates a manager can control directly, one of the determinants is how much the manager can reduce the frequency and time consumed in contacts with his subordinates. 15.___
Of the following, the factor which LEAST influences the number and direction of these contacts is:

A. How well the manager delegates authority
B. The rate at which the organization is changing
C. The control techniques used by the manager
D. Whether the activity is line or staff

16. Systematic rotation of employees through lateral transfer within a government organization to provide for managerial development is 16.___

A. *good,* because systematic rotation develops specialists who learn to do many jobs well
B. *bad,* because the outsider upsets the status quo of the existing organization
C. *good,* because rotation provides challenge and organizational flexibility
D. *bad,* because it is upsetting to employees to be transferred within a service

17. Assume that you are required to provide an evaluation of the performance of your subordinates. 17.___
Of the following factors, it is MOST important that the performance evaluation include a rating of each employees

A. initiative B. productivity C. intelligence D. personality

18. When preparing performance evaluations of your subordinates, *one* way to help assure that you are rating each employee fairly is to 18.___

A. prepare a list of all employees and all the rating factors and rate all employees on one rating factor before going on to the next factor
B. prepare a list of all your employees and all the rating factors and rate each employee on all factors before going on to the next employee
C. discuss all the ratings you anticipate giving with another supervisor in order to obtain an unbiased opinion
D. discuss each employee with his co-workers in order to obtain peer judgment of worth before doing any rating

19. A managerial plan which would include the GREATEST control is a plan which is 19.___

A. spontaneous and geared to each new job that is received
B. detailed and covering an extended time period
C. long-range and generalized, allowing for various interpretations
D. specific and prepared daily

20. Assume that you are preparing a report which includes statistical data covering increases in budget allocations of four agencies for the past ten years. 20.____
For you to represent the statistical data pictorially or graphically within the report is a

A. *poor idea,* because you should be able to make statistical data understandable through the use of words
B. *good idea,* because it is easier for the reader to understand pictorial representation rather than quantities of words conveying statistical data
C. *poor idea,* because using pictorial representation in a report may make the report too expensive to print
D. *good idea,* because a pictorial representation makes the report appear more attractive than the use of many words to convey the statistical data

---

KEY (CORRECT ANSWERS)

1.	C	11.	A
2.	A	12.	B
3.	B	13.	C
4.	D	14.	A
5.	D	15.	D
6.	D	16.	C
7.	D	17.	B
8.	B	18.	A
9.	C	19.	B
10.	C	20.	B

TEST 2

DIRECTIONS: Each question or incomplete statement is followed by several suggested answers or completions. Select the one that BEST answers the question or completes the statement. *PRINT THE LETTER OF THE CORRECT ANSWER IN THE SPACE AT THE RIGHT.*

1. Research studies have shown that supervisors of groups with high production records USUALLY 1.___

   A. give detailed instructions, constantly check on progress, and insist on approval of all decisions before implementation
   B. do considerable paperwork and other work similar to that performed by subordinates
   C. think of themselves as team members on the same level as others in the work group
   D. perform tasks traditionally associated with managerial functions

2. Mr. Smith, a bureau chief, is summoned by his agency's head in a conference to discuss Mr. Jones, an accountant who works in one of the divisions of his bureau. Mr. Jones has committed an error of such magnitude as to arouse the agency head's concern. 2.___
   After agreeing with the other conferees that a severe reprimand would be the appropriate punishment, Mr. Smith should

   A. arrange for Mr. Jones to explain the reasons for his error to the agency head
   B. send a memorandum to Mr. Jones, being careful that the language emphasizes the nature of the error rather than Mr. Jones' personal faults
   C. inform Mr. Jones' immediate supervisor of the conclusion reached at the conference, and let the supervisor take the necessary action
   D. suggest to the agency head that no additional action be taken against Mr. Jones because no further damage will be caused by the error

3. Assume that Ms. Thomson, a unit chief, has determined that the findings of an internal audit have been seriously distorted as a result of careless errors. The audit had been performed by a group of auditors in her unit and the errors were overlooked by the associate accountant in charge of the audit. Ms. Thomson has decided to delay discussing the matter with the associate accountant and the staff who performed the audit until she verifies certain details, which may require prolonged investigation. 3.___
   Ms. Thomson's method of handling this situation is

   A. *appropriate;* employees should not be accused of wrongdoing until all the facts have been determined
   B. *inappropriate;* the employees involved may assume that the errors were considered unimportant
   C. *appropriate;* employees are more likely to change their behavior as a result of disciplinary action taken after a *cooling off* period
   D. *inappropriate;* the employees involved may have forgotten the details and become emotionally upset when confronted with the facts

4. After studying the financial situation in his agency, an administrative accountant decides to recommend centralization of certain accounting functions which are being performed in three different bureaus of the organization. 4.____
The one of the following which is *most likely* to be a DISADVANTAGE if this recommendation is implemented is that

   A. there may be less coordination of the accounting procedure because central direction is not so close to the day-to-day problems as the personnel handling them in each specialized accounting unit
   B. the higher management levels would not be able to make emergency decisions in as timely a manner as the more involved, lower-level administrators who are closer to the problem
   C. it is more difficult to focus the attention of the top management in order to resolve accounting problems because of the many other activities top management is involved in at the same time
   D. the accuracy of upward and inter-unit communication may be reduced because centralization may require insertion of more levels of administration in the chain of command

5. Of the following assumptions about the role of conflict in an organization, the *one* which is the MOST accurate statement of the approach of modern management theorists is that conflict 5.____

   A. can usually be avoided or controlled
   B. serves as a vital element in organizational change
   C. works against attainment of organizational goals
   D. provides a constructive outlet for problem employees

6. Which of the following is generally regarded as the BEST approach for a supervisor to follow in handling grievances brought by subordinates? 6.____

   A. Avoid becoming involved personally
   B. Involve the union representative in the first stage of discussion
   C. Settle the grievance as soon as possible
   D. Arrange for arbitration by a third party

7. Assume that supervisors of similar-sized accounting units in city, state, and federal offices were interviewed and observed at their work. It was found that the ways they acted in and viewed their roles tended to be very similar, regardless of who employed them. 7.____
Which of the following is the BEST explanation of this similarity?

   A. A supervisor will ordinarily behave in conformance to his own self-image
   B. Each role in an organization, including the supervisory role, calls for a distinct type of personality
   C. The supervisory role reflects an exceptionally complex pattern of human response
   D. The general nature of the duties and responsibilities of the supervisory position determines the role

8. Which of the following is NOT consistent with the findings of recent research about the characteristics of successful top managers? 8.___

A. They are *inner-directed* and not overly concerned with pleasing others
B. They are challenged by situations filled with high risk and ambiguity
C. They tend to stay on the same job for long periods of time
D. They consider it more important to handle critical assignments successfully than to do routine work well

9. As a supervisor you have to give subordinate operational guidelines. 9.___
Of the following, the BEST reason for providing them with information about the overall objectives within which their operations fit is that the subordinates will

A. be more likely to carry out the operation according to your expectations
B. know that there is a legitimate reason for carrying out the operation in the way you have prescribed
C. be more likely to handle unanticipated problems that may arise without having to take up your time
D. more likely to transmit the operating instructions correctly to their subordinates

10. A supervisor holds frequent meetings with his staff. 10.___
Of the following, the BEST approach he can take in order to elicit productive discussions at these meetings is for him to

A. ask questions of those who attend
B. include several levels of supervisors at the meetings
C. hold the meetings at a specified time each week
D. begin each meeting with a statement that discussion is welcomed

11. Of the following, the MOST important action that a supervisor can take to increase the productivity of a subordinate is to 11.___

A. increase his uninterrupted work time
B. increase the number of reproducing machines available in the office
C. provide clerical assistance whenever he requests it
D. reduce the number of his assigned tasks

12. Assume that, as a supervisor, you find that you often must countermand or modify your original staff memos. If this practice continues, *which one* of the following situations is MOST likely to occur? The 12.___

A. staff will not bother to read your memos
B. office files will become cluttered
C. staff will delay acting on your memos
D. memos will be treated routinely

13. In making management decisions the committee approach is often used by managers. 13.___
Of the following, the BEST reason for using this approach is to

A. prevent any one individual from assuming too much authority
B. allow the manager to bring a wider range of experience and judgment to bear on the problem
C. allow the participation of all staff members, which will make them feel more committed to the decisions reached
D. permit the rapid transmission of information about decisions reached to the staff members concerned

14. In establishing standards for the measurement of the performance of a management project team, it is MOST important for the project manager to 14.____

A. identify and define the objectives of the project
B. determine the number of people who will be assigned to the project team
C. evaluate the skills of the staff who will be assigned to the project team
D. estimate fairly accurately the length of time required to complete each phase of the project

15. It is virtually impossible to tell an employee either that he is not so good as another employee or that he does not measure up to a desirable level of performance, without having him feel threatened, rejected, and discouraged. 15.____
In accordance with the foregoing observation, a supervisor who is concerned about the performance of the less efficient members of his staff should realize that

A. he might obtain better results by not discussing the quality and quantity of their work with them, but by relying instead on the written evaluation of their performance to motivate their improvement
B. since he is required to discuss their performance with them, he should do so in words of encouragement and in so friendly a manner as to not destroy their morale
C. he might discuss their work in a general way, without mentioning any of the specifics about the quality of their performance, with the expectation that they would understand the full implications of his talk
D. he should make it a point, while telling them of their poor performance, to mention that their work is as good as that of some of the other employees in the unit

16. Some advocates of management-by-objectives procedures in public agencies have been urging that this method of operations be expanded to encompass all agencies of the government, for one or more of the following reasons, not all of which may be correct: 16.____

I. The MBO method is likely to succeed because it embraces the practice of setting near-term goals for the subordinate manager, reviewing accomplishments at an appropriate time, and repeating this process indefinitely
II. Provision for authority to perform the tasks assigned as goals in the MBO method is normally not needed because targets are set in quantitative or qualitative terms and specific times for accomplishment are arranged in short-term, repetitive intervals
III. Many other appraisal-of-performance programs failed because both supervisors and subordinates resisted them, while the MBO approach is not instituted until there is an organizational commitment to it
IV. Personal accountability is clearly established through the MBO approach because verifiable results are set up in the process of formulating the targets

Which of the choices below includes ALL of the foregoing statements that are CORRECT?

A. I and III
B. II and IV
C. I,II,III,IV
D. I,III,IV

17. In preparing an organizational structure, the PRINCIPAL guideline for locating staff units is to place them 17.___

A. all under a common supervisor
B. as close as possible to the activities they serve
C. as close to the chief executive as possible without over-extending his span of control
D. at the lowest operational level

18. The relative importance of any unit in a department can be LEAST reliably judged by the 18.___

A. amount of office space allocated to the unit
B. number of employees in the unit
C. rank of the individual who heads the unit
D. rank of the individual to whom the unit head reports directly

19. Those who favor Planning-Programming-Budgeting Systems (PPBS) as a new method of governmental financial administration emphasize that PPBS 19.___

A. applies statistical measurements which correlate highly with criteria
B. makes possible economic systems analysis, including an explicit examination of alternatives
C. makes available scarce government resources which can be coordinated on a government-wide basis and shared between local units of government
D. shifts the emphasis in budgeting methods to an automated system of data processing

20. The term applied to computer processing which processes data concurrently with a given activity and provides results soon enough to influence the selection of a course of action is 20.___

A. realtime processing
B. batch processing
C. random access processing
D. integrated data processing

KEY (CORRECT ANSWERS)

1.	D	11.	A
2.	C	12.	C
3.	B	13.	B
4.	D	14.	A
5.	B	15.	B
6.	C	16.	D
7.	D	17.	B
8.	C	18.	B
9.	C	19.	B
10.	A	20.	A

INTERPRETING STATISTICAL DATA GRAPHS, CHARTS AND TABLES

EXAMINATION SECTION

TEST 1

DIRECTIONS: Each question or incomplete statement is followed by several suggested answers or completions. Select the one that BEST answers the question or completes the statement. *PRINT THE LETTER OF THE CORRECT ANSWER IN THE SPACE AT THE RIGHT.*

Questions 1-3.

DIRECTIONS: Questions 1 through 3 are to be answered SOLELY on the basis of the following table.

QUARTERLY SALES REPORTED BY MAJOR INDUSTRY GROUPS

DECEMBER 2007 - FEBRUARY 2009

	Reported Sales, Taxable & Non-Taxable (In Millions)				
Industry Groups	12/07-2/08	3/08-5/08	6/08-8/08	9/08-11/08	12/08-2/09
Retailers	2,802	2,711	2,475	2,793	2,974
Wholesalers	2,404	2,237	2,269	2,485	2,512
Manufacturers	3,016	2,888	3,001	3,518	3,293
Services	1,034	1,065	984	1,132	1,092

1. The trend in total reported sales may be described as 1.____

   A. downward
   B. downward and upward
   C. horizontal
   D. upward

2. The two industry groups that reveal a similar seasonal pattern for the period December 2007 through November 2008 are 2.____

   A. retailers and manufacturers
   B. retailers and wholesalers
   C. wholesalers and manufacturers
   D. wholesalers and service

3. Reported sales were at a MINIMUM between 3.____

   A. December 2007 and February 2008
   B. March 2008 and May 2008
   C. June 2008 and August 2008
   D. September 2008 and November 2008

TEST 2

DIRECTIONS: Each question or incomplete statement is followed by several suggested answers or completions. Select the one that BEST answers the question or completes the statement. *PRINT THE LETTER OF THE CORRECT ANSWER IN THE SPACE AT THE RIGHT.*

Questions 1-4.

DIRECTIONS: Questions 1 through 4 are to be answered SOLELY on the basis of the following information.

The income elasticity of demand for selected items of consumer demand in the United States are:

Item	Elasticity
Airline Travel	5.66
Alcohol	.62
Dentist Fees	1.00
Electric Utilities	3.00
Gasoline	1.29
Intercity Bus	1.89
Local Bus	1.41
Restaurant Meals	.75

1. The demand for the item listed below that would be MOST adversely affected by a decrease in income is 1._

   A. alcohol
   B. electric utilities
   C. gasoline
   D. restaurant meals

2. The item whose relative change in demand would be the same as the relative change in income would be 2._

   A. dentist fees
   B. gasoline
   C. restaurant meals
   D. none of the above

3. If income increases by 12 percent, the demand for restaurant meals may be expected to increase by 3._

   A. 9 percent
   B. 12 percent
   C. 16 percent
   D. none of the above

4. On the basis of the above information, the item whose demand would be MOST adversely affected by an increase in the sales tax from 7 percent to 8 percent to be passed on to the consumer in the form of higher prices 4._

   A. would be airline travel
   B. would be alcohol
   C. would be gasoline
   D. cannot be determined

TEST 3

DIRECTIONS: Each question or incomplete statement is followed by several suggested answers or completions. Select the one that BEST answers the question or completes the statement. *PRINT THE LETTER OF THE CORRECT ANSWER IN THE SPACE AT THE RIGHT.*

Questions 1-3.

DIRECTIONS: Questions 1 through 3 are to be answered SOLELY on the basis of the following graphs depicting various relationships in a single retail store.

GRAPH I
RELATIONSHIP BETWEEN NUMBER OF CUSTOMERS STORE AND TIME OF DAY

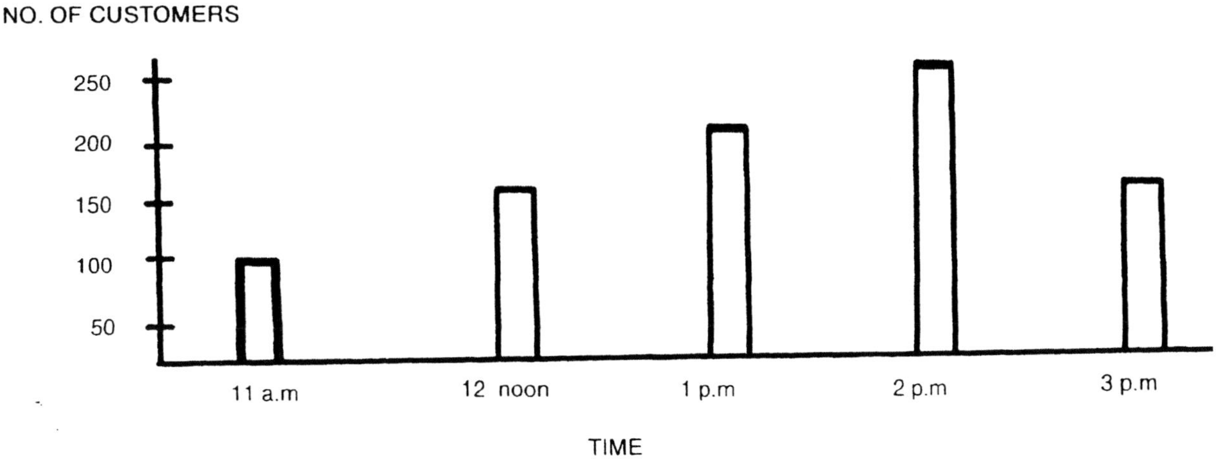

GRAPH II
RELATIONSHIP BETWEEN NUMBER OF CHECK-OUT LANES AVAILABLE IN STORE AND WAIT TIME FOR CHECK-OUT

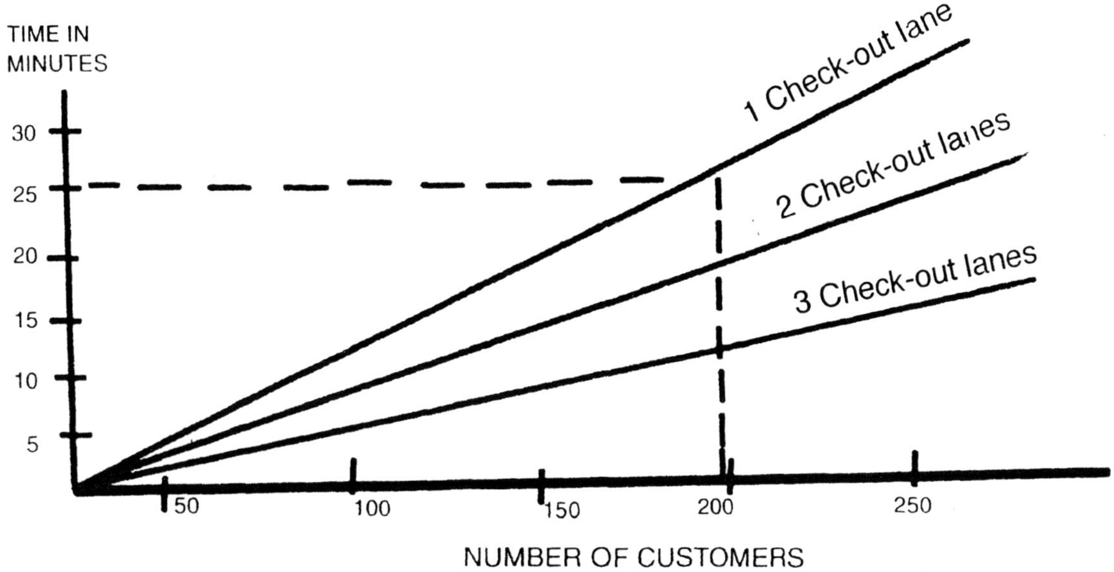

Note the dotted lines in Graph II. They demonstrate that, if there are 200 people in the store and only 1 check-out lane is open, the wait time will be 25 minutes.

1. At what time would a person be most likely NOT to have to wait more than 15 minutes if only one check-out lane is open?

   A. 11 A.M. B. 12 Noon C. 1 P.M. D. 3 P.M.

2. At what time of day would a person have to wait the LONGEST to check out if 3 check-out lanes are available?

   A. 11 A.M. B. 12 Noon C. 1 P.M. D. 2 P.M.

3. The difference in wait times between 1 and 3 check-out lanes at 3 P.M. is MOST NEARLY

   A. 5 B. 10 C. 15 D. 20

TEST 4

DIRECTIONS: Each question or incomplete statement is followed by several suggested answers or completions. Select the one that BEST answers the question or completes the statement. *PRINT THE LETTER OF THE CORRECT ANSWER IN THE SPACE AT THE RIGHT.*

Questions 1-4.

DIRECTIONS: Questions 1 through 4 are to be answered SOLELY on the basis of the graph below.

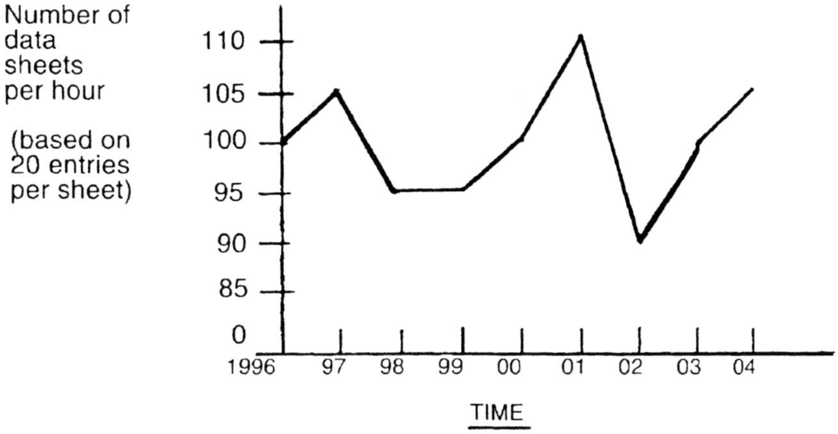

1. Of the following, during what four-year period did the average output of computer operators fall BELOW 100 sheets per hour? 1.____

   A. 1997-00 B. 1998-01 C. 2000-03 D. 2001-04

2. The average percentage change in output over the previous year's output for the years 1999 to 2002 is MOST NEARLY 2.____

   A. 2 B. 0 C. -5 D. -7

3. The difference between the actual output for 2002 and the projected figure based upon the average increase from 1996-2001 is MOST NEARLY 3.____

   A. 18 B. 20 C. 22 D. 24

4. Assume that after constructing the above graph you, an analyst, discovered that the average number of entries per sheet in 2002 was 25 (instead of 20) because of the complex nature of the work performed during that period.
   The average output in cards per hour for the period 2000-03, expressed in terms of 20 items per sheet, would then be MOST NEARLY 4.____

   A. 95 B. 100 C. 105 D. 110

TEST 5

DIRECTIONS: Each question or incomplete statement is followed by several suggested answers or completions. Select the one that BEST answers the question or completes the statement. *PRINT THE LETTER OF THE CORRECT ANSWER IN THE SPACE AT THE RIGHT.*

Questions 1-3.

DIRECTIONS: Questions 1 through 3 are to be answered on the basis of the following data assembled for a cost-benefit analysis.

	Cost	Benefit
No program	0	0
Alternative W	$ 3,000	$ 6,000
Alternative X	$10,000	$17,000
Alternative Y	$17,000	$25,000
Alternative Z	$30,000	$32,000

1. From the point of view of selecting the alternative with the best cost benefit ratio, the BEST alternative is Alternative 1.___

   A. W B. X C. Y D. Z

2. From the point of view of selecting the alternative with the best measure of net benefit, the BEST alternative is Alternative 2.___

   A. W B. X C. Y D. Z

3. From the point of view of pushing public expenditure to the point where marginal benefit equals or exceeds marginal cost, the BEST alternative is Alternative 3.___

   A. W B. X C. Y D. Z

TEST 6

DIRECTIONS: Each question or incomplete statement is followed by several suggested answers or completions. Select the one that BEST answers the question or completes the statement. *PRINT THE LETTER OF THE CORRECT ANSWER IN THE SPACE AT THE RIGHT.*

Questions 1-3.

DIRECTIONS: Questions 1 through 3 are to be answered SOLELY on the basis of the following data.

A series of cost-benefit studies of various alternative health programs yields the following results:

Program	Benefit	Cost
K	30	15
L	60	60
M	300	150
N	600	500

In answering Questions 1 and 2, assume that all programs can be increased or decreased in scale without affecting their individual benefit-to-cost ratios.

1. The benefit-to-cost ratio of Program M is 1.____

   A. 10:1 B. 5:1 C. 2:1 D. 1:2

2. The budget ceiling for one or more of the programs included in the study is set at 75 units. 2.____
   It may MOST logically be concluded that

   A. Programs K and L should be chosen to fit within the budget ceiling
   B. Program K would be the most desirable one that could be afforded
   C. Program M should be chosen rather than Program K
   D. the choice should be between Programs M and K

3. If no assumptions can be made regarding the effects of change of scale, the MOST logical conclusion, on the basis of the data available, is that 3.____

   A. more data are needed for a budget choice of program
   B. Program K is the most preferable because of its low cost and good benefit-to-cost ratio
   C. Program M is the most preferable because of its high benefits and good benefit-to-cost ratio
   D. there is no difference between Programs K and M, and either can be chosen for any purpose

TEST 7

DIRECTIONS: Each question or incomplete statement is followed by several suggested answers or completions. Select the one that BEST answers the question or completes the statement. *PRINT THE LETTER OF THE CORRECT ANSWER IN THE SPACE AT THE RIGHT.*

Questions 1-6.

DIRECTIONS: Questions 1 through 6 are to be answered SOLELY on the basis of the information contained in the charts below which relate to the budget allocations of City X, a small suburban community. The charts depict the annual budget allocations by Department and by expenditures over a five-year period.

CITY X BUDGET IN MILLIONS OF DOLLARS

TABLE I. Budget Allocations By Department

Department	1997	1998	1999	2000	2001
Public Safety	30	45	50	40	50
Health and Welfare	50	75	90	60	70
Engineering	5	8	10	5	8
Human Resources	10	12	20	10	22
Conservation & Environment	10	15	20	20	15
Education & Development	15	25	35	15	15
TOTAL BUDGET	120	180	225	150	180

TABLE II. Budget Allocations by Expenditures

Category	1997	1998	1999	2000	2001
Raw Materials & Machinery	36	63	68	30	98
Capital Outlay	12	27	56	15	18
Personal Services	72	90	101	105	64
TOTAL BUDGET	120	180	225	150	180

1. The year in which the SMALLEST percentage of the total annual budget was allocated to the Department of Education and Development is 1

   A. 1997 B. 1998 C. 2000 D. 2001

2. Assume that in 2000 the Department of Conservation and Environment divided its annual budget into the three categories of expenditures and in exactly the same proportion as the budget shown in Table II for the year 2000. The amount allocated for capital outlay in the Department of Conservation and Environment's 2000 budget was MOST NEARLY ______ million. 2

   A. $2 B. $4 C. $6 D. $10

3. From the year 1998 to the year 2000, the sum of the annual budgets for the Departments of Public Safety and Engineering showed an overall ______ million. 3.____

A. decline; $8
B. increase; $7
C. decline; $15
D. increase; $22

4. The LARGEST dollar increase in departmental budget allocations from one year to the next was in ______ from ______. 4.____

A. Public Safety; 1997 to 1998
B. Health and Welfare; 1997 to 1998
C. Education and Development; 1999 to 2000
D. Human Resources; 1999 to 2000

5. During the five-year period, the annual budget of the Department of Human Resources was GREATER than the annual budget for the Department of Conservation and Environment in ______ of the years. 5.____

A. none
B. one
C. two
D. three

6. If the total City X budget increases at the same rate from 2001 to 2002 as it did from 2000 to 2001, the total City X budget for 2002 will be MOST NEARLY ______ million. 6.____

A. $180
B. $200
C. $210
D. $215

TEST 8

DIRECTIONS: Each question or incomplete statement is followed by several suggested answers or completions. Select the one that BEST answers the question or completes the statement. *PRINT THE LETTER OF THE CORRECT ANSWER IN THE SPACE AT THE RIGHT.*

Questions 1-3.

DIRECTIONS: Questions 1 through 3 are to be answered SOLELY on the basis of the following information.

Assume that in order to encourage Program A, the State and Federal governments have agreed to make the following reimbursements for money spent on Program A, provided the unreimbursed balance is paid from City funds.

During Fiscal Year 2001-2002 - For the first $2 million expended, 50% Federal reimbursement and 30% State reimbursement; for the next $3 million, 40% Federal reimbursement and 20% State reimbursement; for the next $5 million, 20% Federal reimbursement and 10% State reimbursement. Above $10 million expended, no Federal or State reimbursement.

During Fiscal Year 2002-2003 - For the first $1 million expended, 30% Federal reimbursement and 20% State reimbursement; for the next $4 million, 15% Federal reimbursement and 10% State reimbursement. Above $5 million expended, no Federal or State reimbursement.

1. Assume that the Program A expenditures are such that the State reimbursement for Fiscal Year 2001-2002 will be $1 million. 1.___
   Then, the Federal reimbursement for Fiscal Year 2001-2002 will be

   A. $1,600,000 B. $1,800,000
   C. $2,000,000 D. $2,600,000

2. Assume that $8 million were to be spent on Program A in Fiscal Year 2002-2003. 2.___
   The TOTAL amount of unreimbursed City funds required would be

   A. $3,500,000 B. $4,500,000
   C. $5,500,000 D. $6,500,000

3. Assume that the City desires to have a combined total of $6 million spent in Program A during both the Fiscal Year 2001-2002 and the Fiscal Year 2002-2003. 3.___
   Of the following expenditure combinations, the one which results in the GREATEST reimbursement of City funds is ______ in Fiscal Year 2001-2002 and ______ in Fiscal Year 2002-2003.

   A. $5 million; $1 million B. $4 million; $2 million
   C. $3 million; $3 million D. $2 million; $4 million

KEY (CORRECT ANSWERS)

TEST 1

1. D
2. C
3. C

TEST 2

1. B
2. A
3. A
4. D

TEST 3

1. A
2. D
3. B

TEST 4

1. A
2. B
3. C
4. C

TEST 5

1. A
2. C
3. C

TEST 6

1. C
2. D
3. A

TEST 7

1. D
2. A
3. A
4. B
5. B
6. D

TEST 8

1. B
2. D
3. A

PREPARING WRITTEN MATERIAL

PARAGRAPH REARRANGEMENT COMMENTARY

The sentences which follow are in scrambled order. You are to rearrange them in proper order and indicate the letter choice containing the correct answer at the space at the right.

Each group of sentences in this section is actually a paragraph presented in scrambled order. Each sentence in the group has a place in that paragraph; no sentence is to be left out. You are to read each group of sentences and decide upon the best order in which to put the sentences so as to form as well-organized paragraph.

The questions in this section measure the ability to solve a problem when all the facts relevant to its solution are not given.

More specifically, certain positions of responsibility and authority require the employee to discover connections between events sometimes, apparently, unrelated. In order to do this, the employee will find it necessary to correctly infer that unspecified events have probably occurred or are likely to occur. This ability becomes especially important when action must be taken on incomplete information.

Accordingly, these questions require competitors to choose among several suggested alternatives, each of which presents a different sequential arrangement of the events. Competitors must choose the MOST logical of the suggested sequences.

In order to do so, they may be required to draw on general knowledge to infer missing concepts or events that are essential to sequencing the given events. Competitors should be careful to infer only what is essential to the sequence. The plausibility of the wrong alternatives will always require the inclusion of unlikely events or of additional chains of events which are NOT essential to sequencing the given events.

It's very important to remember that you are looking for the best of the four possible choices, and that the best choice of all may not even be one of the answers you're given to choose from.

There is no one right way to these problems. Many people have found it helpful to first write out the order of the sentences, as they would have arranged them, on their scrap paper before looking at the possible answers. If their optimum answer is there, this can save them some time. If it isn't, this method can still give insight into solving the problem. Others find it most helpful to just go through each of the possible choices, contrasting each as they go along. You should use whatever method feels comfortable, and works, for you.

While most of these types of questions are not that difficult, we've added a higher percentage of the difficult type, just to give you more practice. Usually there are only one or two questions on this section that contain such subtle distinctions that you're unable to answer confidently, and you then may find yourself stuck deciding between two possible choices, neither of which you're sure about.

EXAMINATION SECTION
TEST 1

DIRECTIONS: The sentences that follow are in scrambled order. You are to rearrange them in proper order and indicate the letter choice containing the correct answer. *PRINT THE LETTER OF THE CORRECT ANSWER IN THE SPACE AT THE RIGHT.*

1. Below are four statements labeled W., X., Y., and Z. 1.____
   W. He was a strict and fanatic drillmaster.
   X. The word is always used in a derogatory sense and generally shows resentment and anger on the part of the user.
   Y. It is from the name of this Frenchman that we derive our English word, martinet.
   Z. Jean Martinet was the Inspector-General of Infantry during the reign of King Louis XIV.

   The *PROPER* order in which these sentences should be placed in a paragraph is:

   A. X, Z, W, Y B. X, Z, Y, W C. Z, W, Y, X D. Z, Y, W, X

2. In the following paragraph, the sentences which are numbered, have been jumbled. 2.____
   1. Since then it has undergone changes.
   2. It was incorporated in 1955 under the laws of the State of New York.
   3. Its primary purpose, a cleaner city, has, however, remained the same.
   4. The Citizens Committee works in cooperation with the Mayor's Inter-departmental Committee for a Clean City.

   The order in which these sentences should be arranged to form a well-organized paragraph is:

   A. 2, 4, 1, 3 B. 3, 4, 1, 2 C. 4, 2, 1, 3 D. 4, 3, 2, 1

Questions 3-5.

DIRECTIONS: The sentences listed below are part of a meaningful paragraph but they are not given in their proper order. You are to decide what would be the *best order* in which to put the sentences so as to form a well-organized paragraph. Each sentence has a place in the paragraph; there are no extra sentences. You are then to answer questions 3 to 5 inclusive on the basis of your rearrangements of these secrambled sentences into a properly organized paragraph.

In 1887 some insurance companies organized an Inspection Department to advise their clients on all phases of fire prevention and protection. Probably this has been due to the smaller annual fire losses in Great Britain than in the United States. It tests various fire prevention devices and appliances and determines manufacturing hazards and their safeguards. Fire research began earlier in the United States and is more advanced than in Great Britain. Later they established a laboratory specializing in electrical, mechanical, hydraulic, and chemical fields.

3. When the five sentences are arranged in proper order, the paragraph starts with the sentence which begins 3.____

A. "In 1887..." B. "Probably this ..." C. "It tests ..."
D. "Fire research ..." E. "Later they ..."

4. In the last sentence listed above, "they" refers to 4.____

A. insurance companies
B. the United States and Great Britain
C. the Inspection Department
D. clients
E. technicians

5. When the above paragraph is properly arranged, it ends with the words 5.____

A. "... and protection." B. "... the United States."
C. "... their safeguards." D. "... in Great Britain."
E. "... chemical fields."

KEY (CORRECT ANSWERS)

1. C
2. C
3. D
4. A
5. C

TEST 2

DIRECTIONS: In each of the questions numbered 1 through 5, several sentences are given. For each question, choose as your answer the group of numbers that represents the *most logical* order of these sentences if they were arranged in paragraph form. *PRINT THE LETTER OF THE CORRECT ANSWER IN THE SPACE AT THE RIGHT.*

1. 1. It is established when one shows that the landlord has prevented the tenant's enjoyment of his interest in the property leased. 1.____
   2. Constructive eviction is the result of a breach of the covenant of quiet enjoyment implied in all leases.
   3. In some parts of the United States, it is not complete until the tenant vacates within a reasonable time.
   4. Generally, the acts must be of such serious and permanent character as to deny the tenant the enjoyment of his possessing rights.
   5. In this event, upon abandonment of the premises, the tenant's liability for that ceases.

   The CORRECT answer is:

   A. 2, 1, 4, 3, 5 B. 5, 2, 3, 1, 4 C. 4, 3, 1, 2, 5
   D. 1, 3, 5, 4, 2

2. 1. The powerlessness before private and public authorities that is the typical experience of the slum tenant is reminiscent of the situation of blue-collar workers all through the nineteenth century. 2.____
   2. Similarly, in recent years, this chapter of history has been reopened by anti-poverty groups which have attempted to organize slum tenants to enable them to bargain collectively with their landlords about the conditions of their tenancies.
   3. It is familiar history that many of the workers remedied their condition by joining together and presenting their demands collectively.
   4. Like the workers, tenants are forced by the conditions of modern life into substantial dependence on these who possess great political arid economic power.
   5. What's more, the very fact of dependence coupled with an absence of education and self-confidence makes them hesitant and unable to stand up for what they need from those in power.

   The CORRECT answer is:

   A. 5, 4, 1, 2, 3 B. 2, 3, 1, 5, 4 C. 3, 1, 5, 4, 2
   D. 1, 4, 5, 3, 2

3. 1. A railroad, for example, when not acting as a common carrier may contract; away responsibility for its own negligence. 3.____
   2. As to a landlord, however, no decision has been found relating to the legal effect of a clause shifting the statutory duty of repair to the tenant.
   3. The courts have not passed on the validity of clauses relieving the landlord of this duty and liability.
   4. They have, however, upheld the validity of exculpatory clauses in other types of contracts.
   5. Housing regulations impose a duty upon the landlord to maintain leased premises in safe condition.

6. As another example, a bailee may limit his liability except for gross negligence, willful acts, or fraud.

The CORRECT answer is:

A. 2, 1, 6, 4, 3, 5 B. 1, 3, 4, 5, 6, 2 C. 3, 5, 1, 4, 2, 6
D. 5, 3, 4, 1, 6, 2

4. 1. Since there are only samples in the building, retail or consumer sales are generally eschewed by mart occupants, and,in some instances, rigid controls are maintained to limit entrance to the mart only to those persons engaged in retailing. 4.____
2. Since World War I, in many larger cities, there has developed a new type of property, called the mart building.
3. It can, therefore, be used by wholesalers and jobbers for the display of sample merchandise.
4. This type of building is most frequently a multi-storied, finished interior property which is a cross between a retail arcade and a loft building.
5. This limitation enables the mart occupants to ship the orders from another location after the retailer or dealer makes his selection from the samples.

The CORRECT answer is:

A. 2, 4, 3, 1, 5 B. 4, 3, 5, 1, 2 C. 1, 3, 2, 4, 5
D. 1, 4, 2, 3, 5

5. 1. In general, staff-line friction reduces the distinctive contribution of staff personnel. 5.____
2. The conflicts, however, introduce an uncontrolled element into the managerial system.
3. On the other hand, the natural resistance of the line to staff innovations probably usefully restrains over-eager efforts to apply untested procedures on a large scale.
4. Under such conditions, it is difficult to know when valuable ideas are being sacrificed.
5. The relatively weak position of staff, requiring accommodation to the line, tends to restrict their ability to engage .in free, experimental innovation.

The CORRECT answer is:

A. 4, 2, 3, 1, 3 B. 1, 5, 3, 2, 4 C. 5, 3, 1, 2, 4
D. 2, 1, 4, 5, 3

KEY (CORRECT ANSWERS)

1. A
2. D
3. D
4. A
5. B

TEST 3

DIRECTIONS: Questions 1 through 4 consist of six sentences which can be arranged in a logical sequence. For each question, select the choice which places the numbered sentences in the *most logical* sequence. *PRINT THE LETTER OF THE CORRECT ANSWER IN THE SPACE AT THE RIGHT.*

1. 1. The burden of proof as to each issue is determined before trial and remains upon the same party throughout the trial. 1.____
   2. The jury is at liberty to believe one witness' testimony as against a number of contradictory witnesses.
   3. In a civil case, the party bearing the burden of proof is required to prove his contention by a fair preponderance of the evidence.
   4. However, it must be noted that a fair preponderance of evidence does not necessarily mean a greater number of witnesses.
   5. The burden of proof is the burden which rests upon one of the parties to an action to persuade the trier of the facts, generally the jury, that a proposition he asserts is true.
   6. If the evidence is equally balanced, or if it leaves the jury in such doubt as to be unable to decide the controversy either way, judgment must be given against the party upon whom the burden of proof rests.

   The CORRECT answer is:

   A. 3, 2, 5, 4, 1, 6 B. 1, 2, 6, 5, 3, 4 C. 3, 4, 5, 1, 2, 6
   D. 5, 1, 3, 6, 4, 2

2. 1. If a parent is without assets and is unemployed, he cannot be convicted of the crime of non-support of a child. 2.____
   2. The term "sufficient ability" has been held to mean sufficient financial ability.
   3. It does not matter if his unemployment is by choice or unavoidable circumstances.
   4. If he fails to take any steps at all, he may be liable to prosecution for endangering the welfare of a child.
   5. Under the penal law, a parent is responsible for the support of his minor child only if the parent is "of sufficient ability."
   6. An indigent parent may meet his obligation by borrowing money or by seeking aid under the provisions of the Social Welfare Law.

   The CORRECT answer is:

   A. 6, 1, 5, 3, 2, 4 B. 1, 3, 5, 2, 4, 6 C. 5, 2, 1, 3, 6, 4
   D. 1, 6, 4, 5, 2, 3

3. 1. Consider, for example, the case of a rabble rouser who urges a group of twenty people to go out and break the windows of a nearby factory. 3.___
2. Therefore, the law fills the indicated gap with the crime of inciting to riot."
3. A person is considered guilty of inciting to riot when he urges ten or more persons to engage in tumultuous and violent conduct of a kind likely to create public alarm.
4. However, if he has not obtained the cooperation of at least four people, he cannot be charged with unlawful assembly.
5. The charge of inciting to riot was added to the law to cover types of conduct which cannot be classified as either the crime of "riot" or the crime of "unlawful assembly."
6. If he acquires the acquiescence of at least four of them, he is guilty of unlawful assembly even if the project does not materialize.

The CORRECT answer is:

A. 3, 5, 1, 6, 4, 2 B. 5, 1, 4, 6, 2, 3 C. 3, 4, 1, 5, 2, 6
D. 5, 1, 4, 6, 3, 2

4. 1. If, however, the rebuttal evidence presents an issue of credibility, it is for the jury to determine whether the presumption has, in fact, been destroyed. 4.___
2. Once sufficient evidence to the contrary is introduced, the presumption disappears from the trial.
3. The effect of a presumption is to place the burden upon the adversary to come forward with evidence to rebut the presumption.
4. When a presumption is overcome and ceases to exist in the case, the fact or facts which gave rise to the presumption still remain.
5. Whether a presumption has been overcome is ordinarily a question for the court.
6. Such information may furnish a basis for a logical inference.

The CORRECT answer is:

A. 4, 6, 2, 5, 1, 3 B. 3, 2, 5, 1, 4, 6 C. 5, 3, 6, 4, 2, 1
D. 5, 4, 1, 2, 6, 3

KEY (CORRECT ANSWERS)

1. D
2. C
3. A
4. B

PREPARING WRITTEN MATERIAL

EXAMINATION SECTION
TEST 1

DIRECTIONS: Each of the sentences in the Tests that follow may be classified under one of the following four categories:

A. *Faulty* because of incorrect grammar or word usage
B. *Faulty* because of incorrect punctuation
C. *Faulty* because of incorrect capitalization or incorrect spelling
D. *Correct*

Examine each sentence carefully to determine under which of the above four options it is best classified. Then, in the space to the right, print the capital letter preceding the option which is the best of the four suggested above.

(Note that each faulty sentence contains but one type of error. Consider a sentence to be correct if it contains none of the types of errors mentioned, even though there may be other correct ways of expressing the same thought.)

1. He sent the notice to the clerk who you hired yesterday. 1.____

2. It must be admitted, however that you were not informed of this change. 2.____

3. Only the employees who have served in this grade for at least two years are eligible for promotion. 3.____

4. The work was divided equally between she and Mary. 4.____

5. He thought that you were not available at that time. 5.____

6. When the messenger returns; please give him this package. 6.____

7. The new secretary prepared, typed, addressed, and delivered, the notices. 7.____

8. Walking into the room, his desk can be seen at the rear. 8.____

9. Although John has worked here longer than She, he produces a smaller amount of work. 9.____

10. She said she could of typed this report yesterday. 10.____

11. Neither one of these procedures are adequate for the efficient performance of this task. 11.____

12. The typewriter is the tool of the typist; the cashe register, the tool of the cashier. 12.____

13. "The assignment must be completed as soon as possible" said the supervisor. 13.____

14. As you know, office handbooks are issued to all new Employees. 14.____

15. Writing a speech is sometimes easier than to deliver it before an audience. 15.____

16. Mr. Brown our accountant, will audit the accounts next week. 16.____

17. Give the assignment to whomever is able to do it most efficiently. 17.____

18. The supervisor expected either your or I to file these reports. 18.____

KEY (CORRECT ANSWERS)

1.	A	10.	A
2.	B	11.	A
3.	D	12.	C
4.	A	13.	B
5.	D	14.	C
6.	B	15.	A
7.	B	16.	B
8.	A	17.	A
9.	C	18.	A

TEST 2

DIRECTIONS: Each of the sentences in the Tests that follow may be classified under one of the following four categories:

A. *Faulty* because of incorrect grammar or word usage
B. *Faulty* because of incorrect punctuation
C. *Faulty* because of incorrect capitalization or incorrect spelling
D. *Correct*

Examine each sentence carefully to determine under which of the above four options it is best classified. Then, in the space to the right, print the capital letter preceding the option which is the best of the four suggested above.

Note that each faulty sentence contains but one type of error. Consider a sentence to be correct if it contains none of the types of errors mentioned, even though there may be other correct ways of expressing the same thought.)

1. The fire apparently started in the storeroom, which is usually locked. 1.____
2. On approaching the victim two bruises were noticed by this officer. 2.____
3. The officer, who was there examined the report with great care. 3.____
4. Each employee in the office had a seperate desk. 4.____
5. All employees including members of the clerical staff, were invited to the lecture. 5.____
6. The suggested Procedure is similar to the one now in use. 6.____
7. No one was more pleased with the new procedure than the chauffeur. 7.____
8. He tried to persaude her to change the procedure. 8.____
9. The total of the expenses charged to petty cash were high. 9.____
10. An understanding between him and I was finally reached. 10.____

KEY (CORRECT ANSWERS)

1. D
2. A
3. B
4. C
5. B
6. C
7. D
8. C
9. A
10. A

TEST 3

DIRECTIONS: Each of the sentences in the Tests that follow may be classified under one of the following four categories:

A. *Faulty* because of incorrect grammar or word usage
B. *Faulty* because of incorrect punctuation
C. *Faulty* because of incorrect capitalization or incorrect spelling
D. *Correct*

Examine each sentence carefully to determine under which of the above four options it is best classified. Then, in the space to the right, print the capital letter preceding the option which is the best of the four suggested above.

(Note that each faulty sentence contains but one type of error. Consider a sentence to be correct if it contains none of the types of errors mentioned, even though there may be other correct ways of expressing the same thought.)

1. They told both he and *I* that the prisoner had escaped. 1.____

2. Any superior officer, who, disregards the just complaints of his subordinates, is remiss in the performance of his duty. 2.____

3. Only those members of the national organization who resided in the Middle West attended the conference in Chicago. 3.____

4. We told him to give the investigation assignment to whoever was available. 4.____

5. Please do not disappoint and embarass us by not appearing in court. 5.____

6. Although the officer's speech proved to be entertaining, the topic was not relevent to the main theme of the conference. 6.____

7. In February all new officers attended a training course in which they were learned in their principal duties and the fundamental operating procedures of the department. 7.____

8. I personally seen inmate Jones threaten inmates Smith and Green with bodily harm if they refused to participate in the plot. 8.____

9. To the layman, who on a chance visit to the prison observes everything functioning smoothly, the maintenance of prison discipline may seem to be a relatively easily realizable objective. 9.____

10. The prisoners in cell block fourty were forbidden to sit on the cell cots during the recreation hour. 10.____

KEY (CORRECT ANSWERS)

1.	A	6.	C
2.	B	7.	A
3.	C	8.	A
4.	D	9.	D
5.	C	10.	C

TEST 4

DIRECTIONS: Each of the sentences in the Tests that follow may be classified under one of the following four categories:

A. *Faulty* because of incorrect grammar or word usage
B. *Faulty* because of incorrect punctuation
C. *Faulty* because of incorrect capitalization or incorrect spelling
D. *Correct*

Examine each sentence carefully to determine under which of the above four options it is best classified. Then, in the space to the right, print the capital letter preceding the option which is the best of the four suggested above.

(Note that each faulty sentence contains but one type of error. Consider a sentence to be correct if it contains none of the types of errors mentioned, even though there may be other correct ways of expressing the same thought.)

1. I cannot encourage you any. 1.____
2. You always look well in those sort of clothes. 2.____
3. Shall we go to the park? 3.____
4. The man whome he introduced was Mr. Carey. 4.____
5. She saw the letter laying here this morning. 5.____
6. It should rain before the Afternoon is over. 6.____
7. They have already went home. 7.____
8. That Jackson will be elected is evident. 8.____
9. He does not hardly approve of us. 9.____
10. It was he, who won the prize. 10.____

KEY (CORRECT ANSWERS)

1. A	6. C
2. A	7. A
3. D	8. D
4. C	9. A
5. A	10. B

TEST 5

DIRECTIONS: Each of the sentences in the Tests that follow may be classified under one of the following four categories:

DIRECTIONS: Each of the sentences in the Tests that follow may be classified under one of the following four categories:

A. *Faulty* because of incorrect grammar or word usage
B. *Faulty* because of incorrect punctuation
C. *Faulty* because of incorrect capitalization or incorrect spelling
D. *Correct*

Examine each sentence carefully to determine under which of the above four options it is best classified. Then, in the space to the right, print the capital letter preceding the option which is the best of the four suggested above.

Note that each faulty sentence contains but one type of error. Consider a sentence to be correct if it contains none of the types of errors mentioned, even though there may be other correct ways of expressing the same thought.)

1. Shall we go to the park. 1.____
2. They are, alike, in this particular. 2.____
3. They gave the poor man sume food when he knocked on the door. 3.____
4. I regret the loss caused by the error. 4.____
5. The students' will have a new teacher. 5.____
6. They sweared to bring out all the facts. 6.____
7. He decided to open a branch store on 33rd street. 7.____
8. His speed is equal and more than that of a racehorse. 8.____
9. He felt very warm on that Summer day. 9.____
10. He was assisted by his friend, who lives in the next house. 10.____

KEY (CORRECT ANSWERS)

1.	B	6.	A
2.	B	7.	C
3.	C	8.	A
4.	D	9.	C
5.	B	10.	D

TEST 6

DIRECTIONS: Each of the sentences in the Tests that follow may be classified under one of the following four categories:

DIRECTIONS: Each of the sentences in the Tests that follow may be classified under one of the following four categories:

A. *Faulty* because of incorrect grammar or word usage
B. *Faulty* because of incorrect punctuation
C. *Faulty* because of incorrect capitalization or incorrect spelling
D. *Correct*

Examine each sentence carefully to determine under which of the above four options it is best classified. Then, in the space to the right, print the capital letter preceding the option which is the best of the four suggested above.

Note that each faulty sentence contains but one type of error. Consider a sentence to be correct if it contains none of the types of errors mentioned, even though there may be other correct ways of expressing the same thought.)

1. The climate of New York is colder than California. 1.____
2. I shall wait for you on the corner. 2.____
3. Did we see the boy who, we think, is the leader. 3.____
4. Being a modest person, John seldom talks about his invention . 4.____
5. The gang is called the smith street boys. 5.____
6. He seen the man break into the store. 6.____
7. We expected to lay still there for quite a while. 7.____
8. He is considered to be the Leader of his organization. 8.____
9. Although I recieved an invitation, I won't go. 9.____
10. The letter must be here some place. 10.____

KEY (CORRECT ANSWERS)

1. A
2. D
3. B
4. D
5. C
6. A
7. A
8. C
9. C
10. A

TEST 7

DIRECTIONS: Each of the sentences in the Tests that follow may be classified under one of the following four categories:

DIRECTIONS: Each of the sentences in the Tests that follow may be classified under one of the following four categories:

A. *Faulty* because of incorrect grammar or word usage
B. *Faulty* because of incorrect punctuation
C. *Faulty* because of incorrect capitalization or incorrect spelling
D. *Correct*

Examine each sentence carefully to determine under which of the above four options it is best classified. Then, in the space to the right, print the capital letter preceding the option which is the best of the four suggested above.

Note that each faulty sentence contains but one type of error. Consider a sentence to be correct if it contains none of the types of errors mentioned, even though there may be other correct ways of expressing the same thought.)

1. I though it to be he. 1._____
2. We expect to remain here for a long time. 2._____
3. The committee was agreed. 3._____
4. Two-thirds of the building are finished. 4._____
5. The water was froze. 5._____
6. Everyone of the salesmen must supply their own car. 6._____
7. Who is the author of Gone With the Wind? 7._____
8. He marched on and declaring that he would never surrender. 8._____
9. Who shall I say called? 9._____
10. Everyone has left but they. 10._____

KEY (CORRECT ANSWERS)

1.	A	6.	A
2.	D	7.	B
3.	D	8.	A
4.	A	9.	D
5.	A	10.	D

TEST 8

DIRECTIONS: Each of the sentences in the Tests that follow may be classified under one of the following four categories:

DIRECTIONS: Each of the sentences in the Tests that follow may be classified under one of the following four categories:

A. *Faulty* because of incorrect grammar or word usage
B. *Faulty* because of incorrect punctuation
C. *Faulty* because of incorrect capitalization or incorrect spelling
D. *Correct*

Examine each sentence carefully to determine under which of the above four options it is best classified. Then, in the space to the right, print the capital letter preceding the option which is the best of the four suggested above.

Note that each faulty sentence contains but one type of error. Consider a sentence to be correct if it contains none of the types of errors mentioned, even though there may be other correct ways of expressing the same thought.)

1. Who did we give the order to? 1.____
2. Send your order in immediately. 2.____
3. I believe I paid the Bill. 3.____
4. I have not met but one person. 4.____
5. Why aren't Tom, and Fred, going to the dance? 5.____
6. What reason is there for him not going? 6.____
7. The seige of Malta was a tremendous event. 7.____
8. I was there yesterday I assure you. 8.____
9. Your ukelele is better than mine. 9.____
10. No one was there only Mary. 10.____

KEY (CORRECT ANSWERS)

1.	A	6.	A
2.	D	7.	C
3.	C	8.	B
4.	A	9.	C
5.	B	10.	A

TEST 9

DIRECTIONS: In each of the following groups of sentences, one of the four sentences is faulty in grammar, punctuation, or capitalization. Select the incorrect sentence in each case.

1. A. If you had stood at home and done your homework, you would not have failed in arithmetic. 1.____
   B. Her affected manner annoyed every member of the audience.
   C. How will the new law affect our income taxes?
   D. The plants were not affected by the long, cold winter, but they succumbed to the drought of summer.

2. A. He is one of the most able men who have been in the Senate. 2.____
   B. It is he who is to blame for the lamentable mistake.
   C. Haven't you a helpful suggestion to make at this time?
   D. The money was robbed from the blind man's cup.

3. A. The amount of children in this school is steadily increasing. 3.____
   B. After taking an apple from the table, she went out to play.
   C. He borrowed a dollar from me.
   D. I had hoped my brother would arrive before me.

4. A. Whom do you think I hear from every week? 4.____
   B. Who do you think is the right man for the job?
   C. Who do you think I found in the room?
   D. He is the man whom we considered a good candidate for the presidency.

5. A. Quietly the puppy laid down before the fireplace. 5.____
   B. You have made your bed; now lie in it.
   C. I was badly sunburned because I had lain too long in the sun.
   D. I laid the doll on the bed and left the room.

KEY (CORRECT ANSWERS)

1. A
2. D
3. A
4. C
5. A

PHILOSOPHY, PRINCIPLES, PRACTICES AND TECHNICS OF SUPERVISION, ADMINISTRATION, MANAGEMENT AND ORGANIZATION

TABLE OF CONTENTS

TABLE OF CONTENTS (CONTINUED)

PHILOSOPHY, PRINCIPLES, PRACTICES, AND TECHNICS
OF
SUPERVISION, ADMINISTRATION, MANAGEMENT AND ORGANIZATION

I. MEANING OF SUPERVISION

The extension of the democratic philosophy has been accompanied by an extension in the scope of supervision. Modern leaders and supervisors no longer think of supervision in the narrow sense of being confined chiefly to visiting employees, supplying materials, or rating the staff. They regard supervision as being intimately related to all the concerned agencies of society, they speak of the supervisor's function in terms of "growth", rather than the "improvement," of employees.

This modern concept of supervision may be defined as follows:

Supervision is leadership and the development of leadership within groups which are cooperatively engaged in inspection, research, training, guidance and evaluation.

II. THE OLD AND THE NEW SUPERVISION

TRADITIONAL

1. Inspection
2. Focused on the employee
3. Visitation
4. Random and haphazard
5. Imposed and authoritarian
6. One person usually

MODERN

1. Study and analysis
2. Focused on aims, materials, methods, supervisors, employees, environment
3. Demonstrations, intervisitation, workshops, directed reading, bulletins, etc.
4. Definitely organized and planned (scientific)
5. Cooperative and democratic
6. Many persons involved (creative)

III THE EIGHT (8) BASIC PRINCIPLES OF THE NEW SUPERVISION

1. *PRINCIPLE OF RESPONSIBILITY*

Authority to act and responsibility for acting must be joined.

a. If you give responsibility, give authority.
b. Define employee duties clearly.
c. Protect employees from criticism by others.
d. Recognize the rights as well as obligations of employees.
e. Achieve the aims of a democratic society insofar as it is possible within the area of your work.
f. Establish a situation favorable to training and learning.
g. Accept ultimate responsibility for everything done in your section, unit, office, division, department.
h. Good administration and good supervision are inseparable.

2. *PRINCIPLE OF AUTHORITY*

The success of the supervisor is measured by the extent to which the power of authority is not used.

a. Exercise simplicity and informality in supervision.
b. Use the simplest machinery of supervision.
c. If it is good for the organization as a whole, it is probably justified.
d. Seldom be arbitrary or authoritative.
e. Do not base your work on the power of position or of personality.
f. Permit and encourage the free expression of opinions.

3. *PRINCIPLE OF SELF-GROWTH*

The success of the supervisor is measured by the extent to which, and the speed with which, he is no longer needed.

a. Base criticism on principles, not on specifics.
b. Point out higher activities to employees.
c. Train for self-thinking by employees, to meet new situations.
d. Stimulate initiative, self-reliance and individual responsibility.
e. Concentrate on stimulating the growth of employees rather than on removing defects.

4. *PRINCIPLE OF INDIVIDUAL WORTH*

Respect for the individual is a paramount consideration in supervision.

a. Be human and sympathetic in dealing with employees.
b. Don't nag about things to be done.
c. Recognize the individual differences among employees and seek opportunities to permit best expression of each personality.

5. *PRINCIPLE OF CREATIVE LEADERSHIP*

The best supervision is that which is not apparent to the employee.

a. Stimulate, don't drive employees to creative action.
b. Emphasize doing good things.
c. Encourage employees to do what they do best.
d. Do not be too greatly concerned with details of subject or method.
e. Do not be concerned exclusively with immediate problems and activities.
f. Reveal higher activities and make them both desired and maximally possible.
g. Determine procedures in the light of each situation but see that these are derived from a sound basic philosophy.
h. Aid, inspire and lead so as to liberate the creative spirit latent in all good employees.

6. *PRINCIPLE OF SUCCESS AND FAILURE*

There are no unsuccessful employees, only unsuccessful supervisors who have failed to give proper leadership.

a. Adapt suggestions to the capacities, attitudes, and prejudices of employees.
b. Be gradual, be progressive, be persistent.
c. Help the employee find the general principle; have the employee apply his own problem to the general principle.
d. Give adequate appreciation for good work and honest effort.
e. Anticipate employee difficulties and help to prevent them.
f. Encourage employees to do the desirable things they will do anyway.
g. Judge your supervision by the results it secures.

7. *PRINCIPLE OF SCIENCE*

Successful supervision is scientific, objective, and experimental. It is based on facts, not on prejudices.

a. Be cumulative in results.
b. Never divorce your suggestions from the goals of training.
c. Don't be impatient of results.
d. Keep all matters on a professional, not a personal level.
e. Do not be concerned exclusively with immediate problems and activities.
f. Use objective means of determining achievement and rating where possible.

8. *PRINCIPLE OF COOPERATION*

Supervision is a cooperative enterprise between supervisor and employee.

a. Begin with conditions as they are.
b. Ask opinions of all involved when formulating policies.
c. Organization is as good as its weakest link.
d. Let employees help to determine policies and department programs.
e. Be approachable and accessible - physically and mentally.
f. Develop pleasant social relationships.

IV. WHAT IS ADMINISTRATION?

Administration is concerned with providing the environment, the material facilities, and the operational procedures that will promote the maximum growth and development of supervisors and employees. (Organization is an aspect, and a concomitant, of administration.)

There is no sharp line of demarcation between supervision and administration; these functions are intimately interrelated and, often, overlapping. They are complementary activities.

1. *PRACTICES COMMONLY CLASSED AS "SUPERVISORY"*

a. Conducting employees conferences
b. Visiting sections, units, offices, divisions, departments
c. Arranging for demonstrations
d. Examining plans
e. Suggesting professional reading
f. Interpreting bulletins
g. Recommending in-service training courses
h. Encouraging experimentation
i. Appraising employee morale
j. Providing for intervisitation

2. *PRACTICES COMMONLY CLASSIFIED AS "ADMINISTRATIVE"*

a. Management of the office
b. Arrangement of schedules for extra duties
c. Assignment of rooms or areas
d. Distribution of supplies
e. Keeping records and reports
f. Care of audio-visual materials
g. Keeping inventory records
h. Checking record cards and books
i. Programming special activities
j. Checking on the attendance and punctuality of employees

3. *PRACTICES COMMONLY CLASSIFIED AS BOTH "SUPERVISORY" AND "ADMINISTRATIVE"*
    a. Program construction
    b. Testing or evaluating outcomes
    c. Personnel accounting
    d. Ordering instructional materials

V. RESPONSIBILITIES OF THE SUPERVISOR

A person employed in a supervisory capacity must constantly be able to improve his own efficiency and ability. He represents the employer to the employees and only continuous self-examination can make him a capable supervisor.

Leadership and training are the supervisor's responsibility. An efficient working unit is one in which the employees work with the supervisor. It is his job to bring out the best in his employees. He must always be relaxed, courteous and calm in his association with his employees. Their feelings are important, and a harsh attitude does not develop the most efficient employees.

VI. COMPETENCIES OF THE SUPERVISOR

1. Complete knowledge of the duties and responsibilities of his position.
2. To be able to organize a job, plan ahead and carry through.
3. To have self-confidence and initiative.
4. To be able to handle the unexpected situation and make quick decisions.
5. To be able to properly train subordinates in the positions they are best suited for.
6. To be able to keep good human relations among his subordinates.
7. To be able to keep good human relations between his subordinates and himself and to earn their respect and trust.

VII. THE PROFESSIONAL SUPERVISOR-EMPLOYEE RELATIONSHIP

There are two kinds of efficiency: one kind is only apparent and is produced in organizations through the exercise of mere discipline; this is but a simulation of the second, or true, efficiency which springs from spontaneous cooperation. If you are a manager, no matter how great or small your responsibility, it is your job, in the final analysis, to create and develop this involuntary cooperation among the people whom you supervise. For, no matter how powerful a combination of money, machines, and materials a company may have, this is a dead and sterile thing without a team of willing, thinking and articulate people to guide it.

The following 21 points are presented as indicative of the exemplary basic relationship that should exist between supervisor and employee:

1. Each person wants to be liked and respected by his fellow employee and wants to be treated with consideration and respect by his superior.
2. The most competent employee will make an error. However, in a unit where good relations exist between the supervisor and his employees, tenseness and fear do not exist. Thus, errors are not hidden or covered up and the efficiency of a unit is not impaired.
3. Subordinates resent rules, regulations, or orders that are unreasonable or unexplained.
4. Subordinates are quick to resent unfairness, harshness, injustices and favoritism.
5. An employee will accept responsibility if he knows that he will be complimented for a job well done, and not too harshly chastised for failure; that his supervisor will check the cause of the failure, and, if it was the supervisor's fault, he will assume the blame therefore. If it was the employee's fault, his supervisor will explain the correct method or means of handling the responsibility.

6. An employee wants to receive credit for a suggestion he has made, that is used. If a suggestion cannot be used, the employee is entitled to an explanation. The supervisor should not say "no" and close the subject.
7. Fear and worry slow up a worker's ability. Poor working environment can impair his physical and mental health. A good supervisor avoids forceful methods, threats and arguments to get a job done.
8. A forceful supervisor is able to train his employees individually and as a team, and is able to motivate them in the proper channels.
9. A mature supervisor is able to properly evaluate his subordinates and to keep them happy and satisfied.
10. A sensitive supervisor will never patronize his subordinates.
11. A worthy supervisor will respect his employees' confidences.
12. Definite and clear-cut responsibilities should be assigned to each executive.
13. Responsibility should always be coupled with corresponding authority.
14. No change should be made in the scope or responsibilities of a position without a definite understanding to that effect on the part of all persons concerned.
15. No executive or employee, occupying a single position in the organization, should be subject to definite orders from more than one source.
16. Orders should never be given to subordinates over the head of a responsible executive. Rather than do this, the officer in question should be supplanted.
17. Criticisms of subordinates should, whoever possible, be made privately, and in no case should a subordinate be criticized in the presence of executives or employees of equal or lower rank.
18. No dispute or difference between executives or employees as to authority or responsibilities should be considered too trivial for prompt and careful adjudication.
19. Promotions, wage changes, and disciplinary action should always be approved by the executive immediately superior to the one directly responsible.
20. No executive or employee should ever be required, or expected, to be at the same time an assistant to, and critic of, another.
21. Any executive whose work is subject to regular inspection should, whever practicable, be given the assistance and facilities necessary to enable him to maintain an independent check of the quality of his work.

VIII. MINI-TEXT IN SUPERVISION, ADMINISTRATION, MANAGEMENT, AND ORGANIZATION

A. BRIEF HIGHLIGHTS

Listed concisely and sequentially are major headings and important data in the field for quick recall and review.

1. *LEVELS OF MANAGEMENT*

Any organization of some size has several levels of management. In terms of a ladder the levels are:

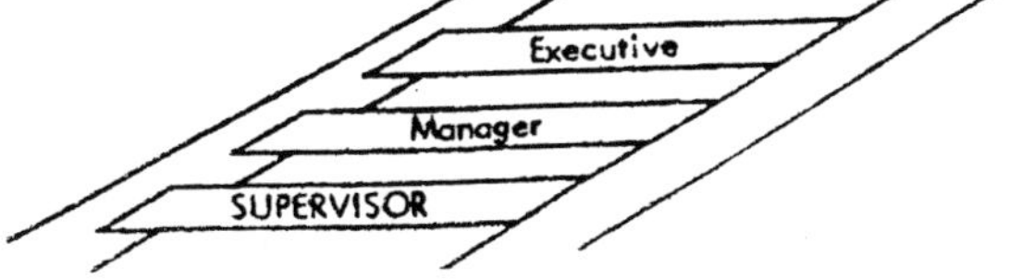

The first level is very important because it is the beginning point of management leadership.

2. *WHAT THE SUPERVISOR MUST LEARN*

A supervisor must learn to:

(1) Deal with people and their differences
(2) Get the job done through people
(3) Recognize the problems when they exist
(4) Overcome obstacles to good performance
(5) Evaluate the performance of people
(6) Check his own performance in terms of accomplishment

3. *A DEFINITION OF SUPERVISOR*

The term supervisor means any individual having authority, in the interests of the employer, to hire, transfer, suspend, lay-off, recall, promote, discharge, assign, reward, or discipline other employees or responsibility to direct them, or to adjust their grievances, or effectively to recommend such action, if, in connection with the foregoing, exercise of such authority is not of a merely routine or clerical nature but requires the use of independent judgment.

4. *ELEMENTS OF THE TEAM CONCEPT*

What is involved in teamwork? The component parts are:

(1) Members	(3) Goals	(5) Cooperation
(2) A leader	(4) Plans	(6) Spirit

5. *PRINCIPLES OF ORGANIZATION*

(1) A team member must know what his job is.
(2) Be sure that the nature and scope of a job are understood.
(3) Authority and responsibility should be carefully spelled out.
(4) A supervisor should be permitted to make the maximum number of decisions affecting his employees.
(5) Employees should report to only one supervisor.
(6) A supervisor should direct only as many employees as he can handle effectively.
(7) An organization plan should be flexible.
(8) Inspection and performance of work should be separate.
(9) Organizational problems should receive immediate attention.
(10) Assign work in line with ability and experience.

6. *THE FOUR IMPORTANT PARTS OF EVERY JOB*

(1) Inherent in every job is the *accountability* for results.
(2) A second set of factors in every job is *responsibilities.*
(3) Along with duties and responsibilities one must have the *authority* to act within certain limits without obtaining permission to proceed.
(4) No job exists in a vacuum. The supervisor is surrounded by key *relationships.*

7. *PRINCIPLES OF DELEGATION*

Where work is delegated for the first time, the supervisor should think in terms of these questions:

(1) Who is best qualified to do this?
(2) Can an employee improve his abilities by doing this?
(3) How long should an employee spend on this?
(4) Are there any special problems for which he will need guidance?
(5) How broad a delegation can I make?

8. *PRINCIPLES OF EFFECTIVE COMMUNICATIONS*
   (1) Determine the media
   (2) To whom directed?
   (3) Identification and source authority
   (4) Is communication understood?

9. *PRINCIPLES OF WORK IMPROVEMENT*
   (1) Most people usually do only the work which is assigned to them
   (2) Workers are likely to fit assigned work into the time available to perform it
   (3) A good workload usually stimulates output
   (4) People usually do their best work when they know that results will be reviewed or inspected
   (5) Employees usually feel that someone else is responsible for conditions of work, workplace layout, job methods, type of tools/equipment, and other such factors
   (6) Employees are usually defensive about their job security
   (7) Employees have natural resistance to change
   (8) Employees can support or destroy a supervisor
   (9) A supervisor usually earns the respect of his people through his personal example of diligence and efficiency

10. *AREAS OF JOB IMPROVEMENT*
    The areas of job improvement are quite numerous, but the most common ones which a supervisor can identify and utilize are:

(1) Departmental layout	(5) Work methods
(2) Flow of work	(6) Materials handling
(3) Workplace layout	(7) Utilization
(4) Utilization of manpower	(8) Motion economy

11. *SEVEN KEY POINTS IN MAKING IMPROVEMENTS*
    (1) Select the job to be improved
    (2) Study how it is being done now
    (3) Question the present method
    (4) Determine actions to be taken
    (5) Chart proposed method
    (6) Get approval and apply
    (7) Solicit worker participation

12. *CORRECTIVE TECHNIQUES OF JOB IMPROVEMENT*

Specific Problems	General Improvement	Corrective Techniques
(1) Size of workload	(1) Departmental layout	(1) Study with scale model
(2) Inability to meet schedules	(2) Flow of work	(2) Flow chart study
(3) Strain and fatigue	(3) Work plan layout	(3) Motion analysis
(4) Improper use of men and skills	(4) Utilization of manpower	(4) Comparison of units produced to standard allowance
(5) Waste, poor quality, unsafe conditions	(5) Work methods	(5) Methods analysis
(6) Bottleneck conditions that hinder output	(6) Materials handling	(6) Flow chart & equipment study
(7) Poor utilization of equipment and machine	(7) Utilization of equipment	(7) Down time vs. running time
(8) Efficiency and productivity of labor	(8) Motion economy	(8) Motion analysis

13. A *PLANNING CHECKLIST*

(1) Objectives	(6) Resources	(11) Safety
(2) Controls	(7) Manpower	(12) Money
(3) Delegations	(8) Equipment	(13) Work
(4) Communications	(9) Supplies and materials	(14) Timing of improvements
(5) Resources	(10) Utilization of time	

14. *FIVE CHARACTERISTICS OF GOOD DIRECTIONS*

In order to get results, directions must be:

(1) Possible of accomplishment	(3) Related to mission	(5) Unmistakably clear
(2) Agreeable with worker interests	(4) Planned and complete	

15. *TYPES OF DIRECTIONS*

(1) Demands or direct orders	(3) Suggestion or implication
(2) Requests	(4) Volunteering

16. *CONTROLS*

A typical listing of the overall areas in which the supervisor should establish controls might be:

(1) Manpower	(3) Quality of work	(5) Time	(7) Money
(2) Materials	(4) Quantity of work	(6) Space	(8) Methods

17. *ORIENTING THE NEW EMPLOYEE*

(1) Prepare for him	(3) Orientation for the job
(2) Welcome the new employee	(4) Follow-up

18. *CHECKLIST FOR ORIENTING NEW EMPLOYEES*

	Yes	No
(1) Do your appreciate the feelings of new employees when they first report for work?	____	____
(2) Are you aware of the fact that the new employee must make a big adjustment to his job?	____	____
(3) Have you given him good reasons for liking the job and the organization?	____	____
(4) Have you prepared for his first day on the job?		
(5) Did you welcome him cordially and make him feel needed?		
(6) Did you establish rapport with him so that he feels free to talk and discuss matters with you?	____	____
(7) Did you explain his job to him and his relationship to you?	____	____
(8) Does he know that his work will be evaluated periodically on a basis that is fair and objective?	____	____
(9) Did you introduce him to his fellow workers in such a way that they are likely to accept him?	____	____
(10) Does he know what employee benefits he will receive?		
(11) Does he understand the importance of being on the job and what to do if he must leave his duty station?	____	____
(12) Has he been impressed with the importance of accident prevention and safe practice?	____	____
(13) Does he generally know his way around the department?	____	____
(14) Is he under the guidance of a sponsor who will teach the right ways of doing things?	____	____
(15) Do you plan to follow-up so that he will continue to adjust successfully to his job?	____	____

19. *PRINCIPLES OF LEARNING*
(1) Motivation (2) Demonstration or explanation (3) Practice

20. *CAUSES OF POOR PERFORMANCE*
(1) Improper training for job
(2) Wrong tools
(3) Inadequate directions
(4) Lack of supervisory follow-up
(5) Poor communications
(6) Lack of standards of performance
(7) Wrong work habits
(8) Low morale
(9) Other

21. *FOUR MAJOR STEPS IN ON-THE-JOB INSTRUCTION*
(1) Prepare the worker
(2) Present the operation
(3) Tryout performance
(4) Follow-up

22. *EMPLOYEES WANT FIVE THINGS*
(1) Security (2) Opportunity (3) Recognition (4) Inclusion (5) Expression

23. *SOME DON'TS IN REGARD TO PRAISE*
(1) Don't praise a person for something he hasn't done
(2) Don't praise a person unless you can be sincere
(3) Don't be sparing in praise just because your superior withholds it from you
(4) Don't let too much time elapse between good performance and recognition of it

24. *HOW TO GAIN YOUR WORKERS' CONFIDENCE*
Methods of developing confidence include such things as:
(1) Knowing the interests, habits, hobbies of employees
(2) Admitting your own inadequacies
(3) Sharing and telling of confidence in others
(4) Supporting people when they are in trouble
(5) Delegating matters that can be well handled
(6) Being frank and straightforward about problems and working conditions
(7) Encouraging others to bring their problems to you
(8) Taking action on problems which impede worker progress

25. *SOURCES OF EMPLOYEE PROBLEMS*
On-the-job causes might be such things as:
(1) A feeling that favoritism is exercised in assignments
(2) Assignment of overtime
(3) An undue amount of supervision
(4) Changing methods or systems
(5) Stealing of ideas or trade secrets
(6) Lack of interest in job
(7) Threat of reduction in force
(8) Ignorance or lack of communications
(9) Poor equipment
(10) Lack of knowing how supervisor feels toward employee
(11) Shift assignments

Off-the-job problems might have to do with:
(1) Health (2) Finances (3) Housing (4) Family

26. *THE SUPERVISOR'S KEY TO DISCIPLINE*

There are several key points about discipline which the supervisor should keep in mind:

(1) Job discipline is one of the disciplines of life and is directed by the supervisor.
(2) It is more important to correct an employee fault than to fix blame for it.
(3) Employee performance is affected by problems both on the job and off.
(4) Sudden or abrupt changes in behavior can be indications of important employee problems.
(5) Problems should be dealt with as soon as possible after they are identified.
(6) The attitude of the supervisor may have more to do with solving problems than the techniques of problem solving.
(7) Correction of employee behavior should be resorted to only after the supervisor is sure that training or counseling will not be helpful.
(8) Be sure to document your disciplinary actions.
(9) Make sure that you are disciplining on the basis of facts rather than personal feelings.
(10) Take each disciplinary step in order, being careful not to make snap judgments, or decisions based on impatience.

27. *FIVE IMPORTANT PROCESSES OF MANAGEMENT*

(1) Planning
(2) Organizing
(3) Scheduling
(4) Controlling
(5) Motivating

28. *WHEN THE SUPERVISOR FAILS TO PLAN*

(1) Supervisor creates impression of not knowing his job
(2) May lead to excessive overtime
(3) Job runs itself -- supervisor lacks control
(4) Deadlines and appointments missed
(5) Parts of the work go undone
(6) Work interrupted by emergencies
(7) Sets a bad example
(8) Uneven workload creates peaks and valleys
(9) Too much time on minor details at expense of more important tasks

29. *FOURTEEN GENERAL PRINCIPLES OF MANAGEMENT*

(1) Division of work
(2) Authority and responsibility
(3) Discipline
(4) Unity of command
(5) Unity of direction
(6) Subordination of individual interest to general interest
(7) Remuneration of personnel
(8) Centralization
(9) Scalar chain
(10) Order
(11) Equity
(12) Stability of tenure of personnel
(13) Initiative
(14) Esprit de corps

30. *CHANGE*

Bringing about change is perhaps attempted more often, and yet less well understood, than anything else the supervisor does. How do people generally react to change? (People tend to resist change that is imposed upon them by other individuals or circumstances.

Change is characteristic of every situation. It is a part of every real endeavor where the efforts of people are concerned.

A. Why do people resist change?

People may resist change because of:

(1) Fear of the unknown
(2) Implied criticism
(3) Unpleasant experiences in the past
(4) Fear of loss of status
(5) Threat to the ego
(6) Fear of loss of economic stability

B. How can we best overcome the resistance to change?

In initiating change, take these steps:

(1) Get ready to sell
(2) Identify sources of help
(3) Anticipate objections
(4) Sell benefits
(5) Listen in depth
(6) Follow up

B. BRIEF TOPICAL SUMMARIES

I. WHO/WHAT IS THE SUPERVISOR?

1. The supervisor is often called the "highest level employee and the lowest level manager."
2. A supervisor is a member of both management and the work group. He acts as a bridge between the two.
3. Most problems in supervision are in the area of human relations, or people problems.
4. Employees expect: Respect, opportunity to learn and to advance, and a sense of belonging, and so forth.
5. Supervisors are responsible for directing people and organizing work. Planning is of paramount importance.
6. A position description is a set of duties and responsibilities inherent to a given position.
7. It is important to keep the position description up-to-date and to provide each employee with his own copy.

II. THE SOCIOLOGY OF WORK

1. People are alike in many ways; however, each individual is unique.
2. The supervisor is challenged in getting to know employee differences. Acquiring skills in evaluating individuals is an asset.
3. Maintaining meaningful working relationships in the organization is of great importance.
4. The supervisor has an obligation to help individuals to develop to their fullest potential.
5. Job rotation on a planned basis helps to build versatility and to maintain interest and enthusiasm in work groups.
6. Cross training (job rotation) provides backup skills.
7. The supervisor can help reduce tension by maintaining a sense of humor, providing guidance to employees, and by making reasonable and timely decisions. Employees respond favorably to working under reasonably predictable circumstances.
8. Change is characteristic of all managerial behavior. The supervisor must adjust to changes in procedures, new methods, technological changes, and to a number of new and sometimes challenging situations.
9. To overcome the natural tendency for people to resist change, the supervisor should become more skillful in initiating change.

III. PRINCIPLES AND PRACTICES OF SUPERVISION

1. Employees should be required to answer to only one superior.
2. A supervisor can effectively direct only a limited number of employees, depending upon the complexity, variety, and proximity of the jobs involved.
3. The organizational chart presents the organization in graphic form. It reflects lines of authority and responsibility as well as interrelationships of units within the organization.
4. Distribution of work can be improved through an analysis using the "Work Distribution Chart."
5. The "Work Distribution Chart" reflects the division of work within a unit in understandable form.
6. When related tasks are given to an employee, he has a better chance of increasing his skills through training.
7. The individual who is given the responsibility for tasks must also be given the appropriate authority to insure adequate results.
8. The supervisor should delegate repetitive, routine work. Preparation of recurring reports, maintaining leave and attendance records are some examples.
9. Good discipline is essential to good task performance. Discipline is reflected in the actions of employees on the job in the absence of supervision.
10. Disciplinary action may have to be taken when the positive aspects of discipline have failed. Reprimand, warning, and suspension are examples of disciplinary action.
11. If a situation calls for a reprimand, be sure it is deserved and remember it is to be done in private.

IV. DYNAMIC LEADERSHIP

1. A style is a personal method or manner of exerting influence.
2. Authoritarian leaders often see themselves as the source of power and authority.
3. The democratic leader often perceives the group as the source of authority and power.
4. Supervisors tend to do better when using the pattern of leadership that is most natural for them.
5. Social scientists suggest that the effective supervisor use the leadership style that best fits the problem or circumstances involved.
6. All four styles -- telling, selling, consulting, joining -- have their place. Using one does not preclude using the other at another time.
7. The theory X point of view assumes that the average person dislikes work, will avoid it whenever possible, and must be coerced to achieve organizational objectives.
8. The theory Y point of view assumes that the average person considers work to be as natural as play, and, when the individual is committed, he requires little supervision or direction to accomplish desired objectives.
9. The leader's basic assumptions concerning human behavior and human nature affect his actions, decisions, and other managerial practices.
10. Dissatisfaction among employees is often present, but difficult to isolate. The supervisor should seek to weaken dissatisfaction by keeping promises, being sincere and considerate, keeping employees informed, and so forth.
11. Constructive suggestions should be encouraged during the natural progress of the work.

V. PROCESSES FOR SOLVING PROBLEMS

1. People find their daily tasks more meaningful and satisfying when they can improve them.
2. The causes of problems, or the key factors, are often hidden in the background. Ability to solve problems often involves the ability to isolate them from their backgrounds. There is some substance to the cliché that some persons "can't see the forest for the trees."
3. New procedures are often developed from old ones. Problems should be broken down into manageable parts. New ideas can be adapted from old ones.

4. People think differently in problem-solving situations. Using a logical, patterned approach is often useful. One approach found to be useful includes these steps:
   (a) Define the problem
   (b) Establish objectives
   (c) Get the facts
   (d) Weigh and decide
   (e) Take action
   (f) Evaluate action

VI. TRAINING FOR RESULTS

1. Participants respond best when they feel training is important to them.
2. The supervisor has responsibility for the training and development of those who report to him.
3. When training is delegated to others, great care must be exercised to insure the trainer has knowledge, aptitude, and interest for his work as a trainer.
4. Training (learning) of some type goes on continually. The most successful supervisor makes certain the learning contributes in a productive manner to operational goals.
5. New employees are particularly susceptible to training. Older employees facing new job situations require specific training, as well as having need for development and growth opportunities.
6. Training needs require continuous monitoring.
7. The training officer of an agency is a professional with a responsibility to assist supervisors in solving training problems.
8. Many of the self-development steps important to the supervisor's own growth are equally important to the development of peers and subordinates. Knowledge of these is important when the supervisor consults with others on development and growth opportunities.

VII. HEALTH, SAFETY, AND ACCIDENT PREVENTION

1. Management-minded supervisors take appropriate measures to assist employees in maintaining health and in assuring safe practices in the work environment.
2. Effective safety training and practices help to avoid injury and accidents.
3. Safety should be a management goal. All infractions of safety which are observed should be corrected without exception.
4. Employees' safety attitude, training and instruction, provision of safe tools and equipment, supervision, and leadership are considered highly important factors which contribute to safety and which can be influenced directly by supervisors.
5. When accidents do occur they should be investigated promptly for very important reasons, including the fact that information which is gained can be used to prevent accidents in the future.

VIII. EQUAL EMPLOYMENT OPPORTUNITY

1. The supervisor should endeavor to treat all employees fairly, without regard to religion, race, sex, or national origin.
2. Groups tend to reflect the attitude of the leader. Prejudice can be detected even in very subtle form. Supervisors must strive to create a feeling of mutual respect and confidence in every employee.
3. Complete utilization of all human resources is a national goal. Equitable consideration should be accorded women in the work force, minority-group members, the physically and mentally handicapped, and the older employee. The important question is: "Who can do the job?"
4. Training opportunities, recognition for performance, overtime assignments, promotional opportunities, and all other personnel actions are to be handled on an equitable basis.

IX. IMPROVING COMMUNICATIONS

1. Communications is achieving understanding between the sender and the receiver of a message. It also means sharing information -- the creation of understanding.
2. Communication is basic to all human activity. Words are means of conveying meanings; however, real meanings are in people.
3. There are very practical differences in the effectiveness of one-way, impersonal, and two-way communications. Words spoken face-to-face are better understood. Telephone conversations are effective, but lack the rapport of person-to-person exchanges. The whole person communicates.
4. Cooperation and communication in an organization go hand in hand. When there is a mutual respect between people, spelling out rules and procedures for communicating is unnecessary.
5. There are several barriers to effective communications. These include failure to listen with respect and understanding, lack of skill in feedback, and misinterpreting the meanings of words used by the speaker. It is also common practice to listen to what we want to hear, and tune out things we do not want to hear.
6. Communication is management's chief problem. The supervisor should accept the challenge to communicate more effectively and to improve interagency and intra-agency communications.
7. The supervisor may often plan for and conduct meetings. The planning phase is critical and may determine the success or the failure of a meeting.
8. Speaking before groups usually requires extra effort. Stage fright may never disappear completely, but it can be controlled.

X. SELF-DEVELOPMENT

1. Every employee is responsible for his own self-development.
2. Toastmaster and toastmistress clubs offer opportunities to improve skills in oral communications.
3. Planning for one's own self-development is of vital importance. Supervisors know their own strengths and limitations better than anyone else.
4. Many opportunities are open to aid the supervisor in his developmental efforts, including job assignments; training opportunities, both governmental and non-governmental -- to include universities and professional conferences and seminars.
5. Programmed instruction offers a means of studying at one's own rate.
6. Where difficulties may arise from a supervisor's being away from his work for training, he may participate in televised home study or correspondence courses to meet his self-develop- ment needs.

XI. TEACHING AND TRAINING

A. The Teaching Process

Teaching is encouraging and guiding the learning activities of students toward established goals. In most cases this process consists in five steps: preparation, presentation, summarization, evaluation, and application.

1. Preparation

Preparation is twofold in nature; that of the supervisor and the employee.

Preparation by the supervisor is absolutely essential to success. He must know what, when, where, how, and whom he will teach. Some of the factors that should be considered are:

(1) The objectives	(5) Employee interest
(2) The materials needed	(6) Training aids
(3) The methods to be used	(7) Evaluation
(4) Employee participation	(8) Summarization

Employee preparation consists in preparing the employee to receive the material. Probably the most important single factor in the preparation of the employee is arousing and maintaining his interest. He must know the objectives of the training, why he is there, how the material can be used, and its importance to him.

2. Presentation

In presentation, have a carefully designed plan and follow it. The plan should be accurate and complete, yet flexible enough to meet situations as they arise. The method of presentation will be determined by the particular situation and objectives.

3. Summary

A summary should be made at the end of every training unit and program. In addition, there may be internal summaries depending on the nature of the material being taught. The important thing is that the trainee must always be able to understand how each part of the new material relates to the whole.

4. Application

The supervisor must arrange work so the employee will be given a chance to apply new knowledge or skills while the material is still clear in his mind and interest is high. The trainee does not really know whether he has learned the material until he has been given a chance to apply it. If the material is not applied, it loses most of its value.

5. Evaluation

The purpose of all training is to promote learning. To determine whether the training has been a success or failure, the supervisor must evaluate this learning.

In the broadest sense evaluation includes all the devices, methods, skills, and techniques used by the supervisor to keep him self and the employees informed as to their progress toward the objectives they are pursuing. The extent to which the employee has mastered the knowledge, skills, and abilities, or changed his attitudes, as determined by the program objectives, is the extent to which instruction has succeeded or failed.

Evaluation should not be confined to the end of the lesson, day, or program but should be used continuously. We shall note later the way this relates to the rest of the teaching process.

B. Teaching Methods

A teaching method is a pattern of identifiable student and instructor activity used in presenting training material.

All supervisors are faced with the problem of deciding which method should be used at a given time.

As with all methods, there are certain advantages and disadvantages to each method.

1. Lecture

The lecture is direct oral presentation of material by the supervisor. The present trend is to place less emphasis on the trainer's activity and more on that of the trainee.

2. Discussion

Teaching by discussion or conference involves using questions and other techniques to arouse interest and focus attention upon certain areas, and by doing so creating a learning situation. This can be one of the most valuable methods because it gives the employees 'an opportunity to express their ideas and pool their knowledge.

3. Demonstration

The demonstration is used to teach how something works or how to do something. It can be used to show a principle or what the results of a series of actions will be. A well-staged demonstration is particularly effective because it shows proper methods of performance in a realistic manner.

4. Performance

Performance is one of the most fundamental of all learning techniques or teaching methods. The trainee may be able to tell how a specific operation should be performed but he cannot be sure he knows how to perform the operation until he has done so.

5. Which Method to Use

Moreover, there are other methods and techniques of teaching. It is difficult to use any method without other methods entering into it. In any learning situation a combination of methods is usually more effective than anyone method alone.

Finally, evaluation must be integrated into the other aspects of the teaching-learning process.

It must be used in the motivation of the trainees; it must be used to assist in developing understanding during the training; and it must be related to employee application of the results of training.

This is distinctly the role of the supervisor.

BASIC FUNDAMENTALS OF A FINANCIAL STATEMENT

TABLE OF CONTENTS

BASIC FUNDAMENTALS OF A FINANCIAL STATEMENT

COMMENTARY

The ability to read and understand a financial statement is a basic requirement for the accountant, auditor, account clerk, bookkeeper, bank examiner. budget examiner, and, of course, for the executive who must manage and administer departmental affairs.

FINANCIAL REPORTS

Are financial reports really as difficult as all that? Well, if you know they are not so difficult because you have worked with them before, this section will be of auxiliary help for you. However, if you find financial statements a bit murky, but realize their great importance to you, we ought to get along fine together. For "mathematics," all we'll use is fourth-grade arithmetic.

Accountants, like all other professionals, have developed a specialized vocabulary. Sometimes this is helpful and sometimes plain confusing (like their practice of calling the income account, "Statement of Profit and Loss," when it is bound to be one or the other). But there are really only a score or so technical terms that you will have to get straight in mind. After that is done, the whole foggy business will begin to clear and in no time at all you'll be able to talk as wisely as the next fellow.

BALANCE SHEET

Look at the sample balance sheet printed on page 2, and we'll have an insight into how it is put together. This particular report is neither the simplest that could be issued, nor the most complicated. It is a good average sample of the kind of report issued by an up-to-date manufacturing company.

Note particularly that the *balance sheet* represents the situation as it stood on one particular day, December 31, not the record of a year's operation. This balance sheet is broken into two parts: on the left are shown *ASSETS* and on the right *LIABILITIES.* Under the asset column, you will find listed the value of things the company owns or are owed to the company. Under liabilities, are listed the things the company owes to others, plus reserves, surplus, and the stated value of the stockholders' interest in the company.

One frequently hears the comment, "Well, I don't see what a good balance sheet is anyway, because the assets and liabilities are always the same whether the company is successful or not."

It is true that they always balance and, by itself, a balance sheet doesn't tell much until it is analyzed. Fortunately, we can make a balance sheet tell its story without too much effort -- often an extremely revealing story, particularly, if we compare the records of several years. ASSETS The first notation on the asset side of the balance sheet is *CURRENT* ASSETS (item 1). In general, current assets include cash and things that can be turned into cash in a hurry, or that, in the normal course of business, will be turned into cash in the reasonably near future, usually within a year.

Item 2 on our sample sheet is *CASH.* Cash is just what you would expect -bills and silver in the till and money on deposit in the bank.

UNITED STATES GOVERNMENT SECURITIES is item 3. The general practice is to show securities listed as current assets at cost or market value, whichever is lower. The figure, for all reasonable purposes, represents the amount by which total cash could be easily increased if the company wanted to sell these securities.

The next entry is *ACCOUNTS RECEIVABLE* (item 4). Here we find the total amount of money owed to the company by its regular business creditors and collectable within the next year. Most of the money is owed to the company by its customers for goods that the company delivered on credit. If this were a department store instead of a manufacturer, what you owed the store on your charge account would be included here. Because some people fail to pay their bills, the company sets up a reserve for doubtful accounts, which it subtracts from all the money owed.

THE ABC MANUFACTURING COMPANY, INC.
CONSOLIDATED BALANCE SHEET – DECEMBER 31

Item		
1. CURRENT ASSETS		
2. Cash		
3. U.S. Government Securities		
4. Accounts Receivable (less reserves)		2,000,000
5. Inventories (at lower of cost or market)		2,000,000
6. Total Current Assets		$7,000,000
7. INVESTMENT IN AFFILIATED COMPANY Not consolidated (at cost, not in excess of net assets)		200,000
8. OTHER INVESTMENTS At cost, less than market		100,000
9. PLANT IMPROVEMENT FUND		550,000
10. PROPERTY, PLANT AND EQUIPMENT: Cost	$8,000,000	
11. Less Reserve for Depreciation	5,000,000	
12. NET PROPERTY		3,000,000
13. PREPAYMENTS		50,000
14. DEFERRED CHARGES		100,000
15. PATENTS AND GOODWILL		100,000
TOTAL		$11,100,000

Item		
16. CURRENT LIABILITIES		
17. Accts. Payable		$ 300,000
18. Accrued Taxes		800,000
19. Accrued Wages, Interest and Other Expenses		370,000
20. Total Current Liabilities		$1,470,000
21. FIRST MORTGAGE SINKING FUND BONDS, 3 1/2% DUE 2002		2,000,000
22. RESERVE FOR CONTINGENCIES		200,000
23. CAPITAL STOCK:		
24. 5% Preferred Stock (authorized and issued 10,000 shares of $100 par value)	$1,000,000	
25. Common stock (authorized and issued 400,000 shares of no par value)	1,000,000	
		2,000,000
26. SURPLUS:		
27. Earned	3,530,000	
28. Capital (arising from sale of common capital stock at price in excess of stated value	1,900,000	
		5,430,000
TOTAL		$11,100,000

Item 5, *INVENTORIES,* is the value the company places on the supplies it owns. The inventory of a manufacturer may contain raw materials that it uses in making the things it sells, partially finished goods in process of manufacture and, finally, completed merchandise that it is ready to sell. Several methods are used to arrive at the value placed on these various items. The most common is to value them at their cost or present market value, whichever is lower. You can be reasonably confident, however, that the figure given is an honest and significant one for the particular industry if the report is certified by a reputable firm of public accountants.

Next on the asset side is *TOTAL CURRENT ASSETS* (item 6). This is an extremely important figure when used in connection with other items in the report, which we will come to presently. Then we will discover how to make total current assets tell their story.

INVESTMENT IN AFFILIATED COMPANY (item 7) represents the cost to our parent company of the capital stock of its *subsidiary* or affiliated company. A subsidiary is simply one company that is controlled by another. Most corporations that own other companies outright, lump the figures in a *CONSOLIDATED BALANCE SHEET.* This means that, under cash, for example, one would find a total figure that represented *all* of the cash of the parent company and of its wholly owned subsidiary. This is a perfectly reasonable procedure because, in the last analysis, all of the money is controlled by the same persons.

Our typical company shows that it has *OTHER INVESTMENTS* (item 8), in addition to its affiliated company. Sometimes good marketable securities other than Government bonds are carried as current assets, but the more conservative practice is to list these other security holdings separately. If they have been bought as a permanent investment, they would always be shown by themselves. "At cost, less than market" means that our company paid $100,000 for these other investments, but they are now worth more.

Among our assets is a *PLANT IMPROVEMENT FUND* (item 9). Of course, this item does not appear in all company balance sheets, but is typical of *special funds* that companies set up for one purpose or another. For example, money set aside to pay off part of the bonded debt of a company might be segregated into a special fund. The money our directors have put aside to improve the plant would often be invested in Government bonds.

FIXED ASSETS

The next item (10), is *PROPERTY, PLANT AND EQUIPMENT,* but it might just as well be labeled *Fixed Assets* as these terms are used more or less interchangeably. Under item 10, the report gives the value of land, buildings, and machinery and such movable things as trucks, furniture, and hand tools. Historically, probably more sins were committed against this balance sheet item than any other.

In olden days, cattlemen used to drive their stock to market in the city. It was a common trick to stop outside of town, spread out some salt for the cattle to make them thirsty and then let them drink all the water they could hold. When they were weighed for sale, the cattlemen would collect cash for the water the stock had drunk. Business buccaneers, taking the cue from their farmer friends, would often "write up" the value of their fixed assets. In other words, they would increase the value shown on the balance sheet, making the capital stock appear to be worth a lot more than it was. *Watered stock* proved a bad investment for most stockholders. The practice has, fortunately, been stopped, though it took major financial reorganizations to squeeze the water out of some securities.

The most common practice today is to list fixed assets at cost. Often, there is no ready market for most of the things that fall under this heading, so it is not possible to give market value. A good report will tell what is included under fixed assets and how it has been valued. If the value has been increased by *write-up* or decreased by *write-down,* a footnote explanation is usually given. A *write-up* might occur, for instance, if the value of real estate increased substantially. A *write-down* might follow the invention of a new machine that put an important part of the company's equipment out of date.

DEPRECIATION

Naturally, all of the fixed property of a company will wear out in time (except, of course, non-agricultural land). In recognition of this fact, companies set up a *RESERVE FOR DEPRECIATION* (item 11). If a truck costs $4,000 and is expected to last four years, it will be depreciated at the rate of $1,000 a year.

Two other terms also frequently occur in connection with depreciation -*depletion* and *obsolescence.* Companies may lump depreciation, depletion, and obsolescence under a single title, or list them separately.

Depletion is a term used primarily by mining and oil companies (or any of the so-called extractive industries). Depletion means exhaust or use up. As the oil or other natural resource is used up, a reserve is set up, to compensate for the natural wealth the company no longer owns. This reserve is set up in recognition of the fact that, as the company sells its natural product, it must get back not only the cost of extracting but also the original cost of the natural resource.

Obsolescence represents the loss in value because a piece of property has gone out of date before it wore out. Airplanes are modern examples of assets that tend to get behind the times long before the parts wear out. (Women and husbands will be familiar with the speed at which ladies' hats "obsolesce.")

In our sample balance sheet we have placed the reserve for depreciation under fixed assets and then subtracted, giving us *NET PROPERTY* (item 12), which we add into the asset column. Sometimes, companies put the reserve for depreciation in the liability column. As you can see, the effect is just the same whether it is *subtracted* from assets or *added* to liabilities.

The manufacturer, whose balance sheet we use, rents a New York showroom and pays his rent yearly, in advance. Consequently, he has listed under assets *PREPAYMENTS* (item 13). This is listed as an asset because he has paid for the use of the showroom, but has not yet received the benefit from its use. The use is something coming to the firm in the following year and, hence, is an asset. The dollar value of this asset will decrease by one-twelfth each month during the coming year.

DEFERRED CHARGES (item 14) represents a type of expenditure similar to prepayment. For example, our manufacturer brought out a new product last year, spending $100,000 introducing it to the market. As the benefit from this expenditure will be returned over months or even years to come, the manufacturer did not think it reasonable to charge the full expenditure against costs during the year. He has *deferred* the charges and will write them off gradually.

INTANGIBLES

The last entry in our asset column is *PATENTS AND GOODWILL* (item 15). If our company were a young one, set up to manufacture some new patented prod uct, it would probably carry its patents at a substantial figure. In fact, *intangibles* of both old and new companies are often of great but generally unmeasurable worth.

Company practice varies considerably in assigning value to intangibles. Procter & Gamble, despite the tremendous goodwill that has been built up for IVORY SOAP, has reduced all of its intangibles to the nominal $1. Some of the big cigarette companies, on the contrary, place a high dollar value on the goodwill their brand names enjoy. Companies that spend a good deal for research and the development of new products are more inclined than others to reflect this fact in the value assigned to patents, license agreements, etc.

LIABILITIES

The liability side of the balance sheet appears a little deceptive at first glance. Several of the entries simply don't sound like liabilities by any ordinary definition of the term.

The first term on the liability side of any balance sheet is usually *CURRENT LIABILITIES* (item 16). This is a companion to the *Current Assets* item across the page and includes all debts that fall due within the next year. The relation between current assets and current liabilities is one of the most revealing things to be gotten from the balance sheet, but we will go into that quite thoroughly later on.

ACCOUNTS PAYABLE (item 17) represents the money that the company owes to its ordinary business creditors -- unpaid bills for materials, supplies, insurance, and the like. Many companies itemize the money they owe in a much more detailed fashion than we have done, but, as you will see, the totals are the most interesting thing to us.

Item 18, *ACCRUED TAXES,* is the tax bill that the company estimates it still owes for the past year. We have lumped all taxes in our balance sheet, as many companies do. However, sometimes you will find each type of tax given separately. If the detailed procedure is followed, the description of the tax is usually quite sufficient to identify the separate items.

Accounts Payable was defined as the money the company owed to its regular business creditors. The company also owes, on any given day, wages to its own employees; interest to its bondholders and to banks from which it may have borrowed money; fees to its attorneys; pensions, etc. These are all totaled under *ACCRUED WAGES, INTEREST AND OTHER EXPENSES* (item 19).

TOTAL CURRENT LIABILITIES (item 20) is just the sum of everything that the company owed on December 31 and which must be paid sometime in the next twelve months.

It is quite clear that all of the things discussed above are liabilities. The rest of the entries on the liability side of the balance sheet, however, do not seem at first glance to be liabilities.

Our balance sheet shows that the company, on December 31, had $2,000,000 of 3 1/2 percent First Mortgage *BONDS* outstanding (item 21). Legally, the money received by a company when it sells bonds is considered a loan to the company. Therefore, it is obvious that the company owes to the bondholders an amount equal to the face value or the *call price* of the bonds it has outstanding. The call price is a figure usually larger than the face value of the bonds at which price the company can *call* the bonds in from the bondholders and pay them off before they ordinarily fall due. The date that often occurs as part of the name of a bond is the date at which the company has promised to pay off the loan from the bondholders.

RESERVES

The next heading, *RESERVE FOR CONTINGENCIES* (item 22), sounds more like an asset than a liability. "My reserves," you might say, "are dollars in the bank, and dollars in the bank are assets."

No one would deny that you have something there. In fact, the corporation treasurer also has his reserve for contingencies balanced by either cash or some kind of unspecified investment on the asset side of the ledger. His reason for setting up a reserve on the liability side of the balance sheet is a precaution against making his financial position seem better than it is. He decided that the company might have to pay out this money during the coming year if certain things happened. If he did not set up the "reserve," his surplus would appear larger by an amount equal to his reserve.

A very large reserve for contingencies or a sharp increase in this figure from the previous year should be examined closely by the investor. Often, in the past, companies tried to hide their true earnings by transferring funds into a contingency reserve. As a reserve looks somewhat like a true liability, stockholders were confused about the real value of their securities. When a reserve is not set up for protection against some very probable loss or expenditure, it should be considered by the investor as part of surplus.

CAPITAL STOCK

Below reserves there is a major heading, *CAPITAL STOCK* (item 23). Companies may have one type of security outstanding, or they may have a dozen. All of the issues that represent shares of ownership are capital, regardless of what they are called on the balance sheet -- preferred stock, preference stock, common stock, founders' shares, capital stock, or something else.

Our typical company has one issue of 5 per cent *PREFERRED STOCK* (item 24). It is called *preferred* because those who own it have a right to dividends and assets before the *common* stockholders -- that is, the holders are in a preferred position as owners. Usually, preferred stockholders do not have a voice in company affairs unless the company fails to pay them dividends at the promised rate. Their rights to dividends are almost always *cumulative.* This simply means that all past dividends must be paid before the other stockholders can receive anything. Preferred stockholders are not creditors of the company so it cannot properly be said that the company *owes* them the value of their holdings. However, in case the company decided to go out of business, preferred stockholders would have a prior claim on anything that was left in the company treasury after all of the creditors, including the bondholders, were paid off. In practice, this right does not always mean much, but it does explain why the book value of their holdings is carried as a liability.

COMMON STOCK (item 25) is simple enough as far as definition is concerned it represents the rights of the ordinary owner of the company. Each company has as many owners as it has stockholders. The proportion of the company that each stockholder owns is determined by the number of shares he has. However, neither the book value of a no-par common stock, nor the par value of an issue that has a given par, can be considered as representing either the original sale price, the market value, or what would be left for the stockholders if the company were liquidated.

A profitable company will seldom be dissolved. Once things have taken such a turn that dissolution appears desirable, the stated value of the stock is generally nothing but a fiction. Even if the company is profitable as a going institution, once it ceases to function even its tangible assets drop in value because there is not usually a ready market for its inventory of raw materials and semi-finished goods, or its plant and machinery.

SURPLUS

The last major heading on the liability side of the balance sheet is *SURPLUS* (item 26). The surplus, of course, is not a liability in the popular sense at all. It represents, on our balance sheet, the difference between the stated value of our common stock and the net assets behind the stock.

Two different kinds of surplus frequently appear on company balance sheets, and our company has both kinds. The first type listed is *EARNED* surplus (item 27). Earned surplus is roughly similar to your own savings. To the corporation, earned surplus is that part of net income which has not been paid to stockholders as dividends. It still *belongs* to you, but the directors have decided that it is best for the company and the stockholders to keep it in the business. The surplus may be invested in the plant just as you might invest part of your savings in your home. It may also be in cash or securities.

In addition to the earned surplus, our company also has a *CAPITAL* surplus (item 28) of $1,900.00, which the balance sheet explains arose from selling the stock at a higher cost per share than is given as its stated value. A little arithmetic shows that the stock is carried on the books at $2.50 a share while the capital surplus amounts to $4.75 a share. From this we know that the company actually received an average of $7.25 net a share for the stock when it was sold.

WHAT DOES THE BALANCE SHEET SHOW?

Before we undertake to analyze the balance sheet figures, a word on just what an investor can expect to learn is in order. A generation or more ago, before present accounting standards had gained wide acceptance, considerable imagination went into the preparation of balance sheets. This, naturally, made the public skeptical of financial reports. Today, there is no substantial ground for skepticism. The certified public accountant, the listing requirements of the national stock exchanges, and the regulations of the Securities and Exchange Commission have, for all practical purposes, removed the grounds for doubting the good faith of financial reports.

The investor, however, is still faced with the task of determining the significance of the figures. As we have already seen, a number of items are based, to a large degree, upon estimates, while others are, of necessity, somewhat arbitrary.

NET WORKING CAPITAL

There is one very important thing that we can find from the balance sheet and accept with the full confidence that we know what we are dealing with. That is net working capital, sometimes simply called working capital.

On the asset side of our balance sheet we have added up all of the current assets and show the total as item 6. On the liability side, item 20 gives the total of current liabilities. *Net working capital* or *net current assets* is the difference left after subtracting current liabilities from current assets. If you consider yourself an investor rather than a speculator, you should always insist that any company in which you invest have a comfortable amount of working capital. The ability of a company to meet its obligations with ease, expand its volume as business expands and take advantage of opportunities as they present themselves, is, to an important degree, determined by its working capital.

Probably the question in your mind is: *"Just what does 'comfortable amount' of working capital mean?"* Well, there are several methods used by analysts to judge whether a particular company has a sound working capital position. The first rough test for an industrial company is to compare the working capital figure with the current liability total. Most analysts say that minimum safety requires that net working capital at least equal current liabilities. Or, put another way, that current assets should be at least twice as large as current liabilities.

There are so many different kinds of companies, however, that this test requires a great deal of modification if it is to be really helpful in analyzing companies in different industries. To help you interpret the *current position* of a company in which you are considering investing, the *current ratio* is more helpful than the dollar total of working capital. The current ratio is current assets divided by current liabilities.

In addition to working capital and current ratio, there are two other ways of testing the adequacy of the current position. *Net quick assets* provide a rigorous and important test of a company's ability to meet its current obligations. Net quick assets are found by taking total current assets (item 6) and subtracting the value of inventories (item 5). A well-fixed industrial company should show a reasonable excess of quick assets over current liabilities..

Finally, many analysts say that a good industrial company should have at least as much working capital (current assets less current liabilities) as the total book value of its bonds and preferred stock. In other words, current liabilities, bonded debt, and preferred stock *altogether* should not exceed the current assets.

INVENTORY AND INVENTORY TURNOVER

In the recent past, there has been much talk of inventories. Many commentators have said that these carry a serious danger to company earnings if management allows them to increase too much. Of course, this has always been true, but present high prices have made everyone more inventory-conscious than usual.

There are several dangers in a large inventory position. In the first place, a sharp drop in price may cause serious losses; also, a large inventory may indicate that the company has accumulated a big supply of unsalable merchandise. The question still remains, however: *"What do we mean by large inventory?"*

As you certainly realize, an inventory is large or small only in terms of the yearly turnover and the type of business. We can discover the annual turnover of our sample company by dividing inventories (item 5) into total annual sales (item "a" on the income account).

It is also interesting to compare the value of the inventory of a company being studied with total current assets. Again, however, there is considerable variation between different types of companies, so that the relationship becomes significant only when compared with similar companies.

NET BOOK VALUE OF SECURITIES

There is one other very important thing that can be gotten from the balance sheet, and that is the net book or equity value of the company's securities. We can calculate the net book value of each of the three types of securities our company has outstanding by a little very simple arithmetic. *Book value means the value at which something is carried on the books of the company.*

The full rights of the bondholders come before any of the rights of the stockholders, so, to find the net book value or net tangible assets backing up the bonds we add together the balance sheet value of the bonds, preferred stock, common stock, reserve, and surplus. This gives us a total of $9,630,000. (We would not include contingency reserve if we were reasonably sure the contingency was going to arise, but, as general reserves are often equivalent to surplus, it is, usually, best to treat the reserve just as though it were surplus.) However, part of this value represents the goodwill and patents carried at $100,000, which is not a tangible item, so, to be conservative, we subtract this amount, leaving $9,530,000 as the total net book value of the bonds. This is equivalent to $4,765 for each $1,000 bond, a generous figure. To calculate the net book value of the preferred stock, we must eliminate the face value of the bonds, and then, following the same procedure, add the value of the preferred stock, common stock, reserve, and surplus, and subtract goodwill. This gives us a total net book value for the preferred stock of $7,530,000 or $753 for each share of $100 par value preferred. This is also very good coverage for the preferred stock, but we must examine current earnings before becoming too enthusiastic about the *value* of any security.

The net book value of the common stock, while an interesting figure, is not so important as the coverage on the senior securities. In case of liquidation, there is seldom much left for the common stockholders because of the normal loss in value of company assets when they are put up for sale, as mentioned before. The book value figure, however, does give us a basis for comparison with other companies. Comparisons of net book value over a period of years also show us if the company is a soundly growing one or, on the other hand, is losing ground. Earnings, however, are our important measure of common stock values, as we will see shortly.

The net book value of the common stock is found by adding the stated value of the common stock, reserves, and surplus and then subtracting patents and goodwill. This gives us a total net book value of $6,530,000. As there are 400,000 shares of common outstanding, each share has a net book value of $16.32. You must be careful not to be misled by book value figures, particularly of common stock. Profitable companies (Coca-Cola, for example) often show a very low net book value and very substantial earnings. Railroads, on the other hand, may show a high book value for their common stock but have such low or irregular earnings that the market price of the stock is much less than its apparent book value. Banks, insurance companies, and investment -trusts are exceptions to what we have said about common stock net book value. As their assets are largely liquid (i.e., cash, accounts receivable, and marketable securities), the book value of their common stock sometimes indicates its value very accurately.

PROPORTION OF BONDS, PREFERRED AND COMMON STOCK

Before investing, you will want to know the proportion of each kind of security issued by the company you are considering. A high proportion of bonds reduces the attractiveness of both the preferred and common stock, while too large an amount of preferred detracts from the value of the common.

The *bond ratio* is found by dividing the face value of the bonds (item 21), or $2,000,000, by the total value of the bonds, preferred stock, common stock, reserve, and surplus, or $9,630,000. This shows that bonds amount to about 20 per cent of the total of bonds, capital, and surplus.

The *preferred stock ratio* is found in the same way, only we divide the stated value of the preferred stock by the total of the other five items. Since we have half as much preferred stock as we have bonds, the preferred ratio is roughly 10.

Naturally, the *common stock ratio* will be the difference between 100 per cent and the totals of the bonds and preferred, or 70 per cent in our sample company. You will want to remember that the most valuable method of determining the common stock ratio is in combination with reserve and surplus. The surplus, as we have noted, is additional backing for the common stock and usually represents either original funds paid in to the company in excess of the stated value of the common stock (capital surplus), or undistributed earnings (earned surplus).

Most investment analysts carefully examine industrial companies that have more than about a quarter of their capitalization represented by bonds, while common stock should total at least as much as all senior securities (bonds and preferred issues). When this is not the case, companies often find it difficult to raise new capital. Banks don't like to lend them money because of the already large debt, and it is sometimes difficult to sell common stock because of all the bond interest or preferred dividends that must be paid before anything is available for the common stockholder.

Railroads and public utility companies are exceptions to most of the rules of thumb that we use in discussing The ABC Manufacturing Company, Inc. Their situation is different because of the tremendous amounts of money they have invested in their fixed assets., their small inventories and the ease with which they can collect their receivables. Senior securities of railroads and utility companies frequently amount to more than half of their capitalization. Speculators often interest themselves in companies that have a high proportion of debt or preferred stock because of the *leverage factor.* A simple illustration will show why. Let us take, for example, a company with $10,000,000 of 4 per cent bonds outstanding. If the company is earning $440,000 before bond interest, there will be only $40,000 left for the common stock ($10,000,000 at 4% equals $400,000). However, an increase of only 10 per cent in earnings (to $484,000) will leave $84,000 for common stock dividends, or an increase of more than 100 per cent. If there is only a small common issue, the increase in earnings per share would appear very impressive.

You have probably already noticed that a decline of 10 per cent in earnings would not only wipe out everything available for the common stock, but result in the company being unable to cover its full interest on its bonds without dipping into surplus. This is the great danger of so-called high leverage stocks and also illustrates the fundamental weakness of companies that have a disproportionate amount of debt or preferred stock. Investors would do well to steer clear of them. Speculators, however, will continue to be fascinated by the market opportunities they offer.

THE INCOME ACCOUNT

The fundamental soundness of a company, as shown by its balance sheet, is important to investors, but of even greater interest is the record of its operation. Its financial structure shows much of its ability to weather storms and pick up speed when times are good. It is the income record, however, that shows us how a company is actually doing and gives us our best guide to the future.

The *Consolidated Income and Earned Surplus* account of our company is stated on the next page. Follow the items given there and we will find out just how our company earned its money, what it did with its earnings, and what it all means in terms of our three classes of securities. We have used a combined income and surplus account because that is the form most frequently followed by industrial companies. However, sometimes the two statements are given separately. Also, a variety of names are used to describe this same part of the financial report. Sometimes it is called profit and loss account, sometimes *record of earnings,* and, often, simply *income account.* They are all the same thing.

The details that you will find on different income statements also vary a great deal. Some companies show only eight or ten separate items, while others will give a page or more of closely spaced entries that break down each individual type of revenue or cost. We have tried to strike a balance between extremes; give the major items that are in most income statements, omitting details that are only interesting to the expert analyst.

The most important source of revenue always makes up the first item on the income statement. In our company, it is *Net Sales* (item "a"). If it were a railroad or a utility instead of a manufacturer, this item would be called *gross revenues.* In any case, it represents the money paid into the company by its customers. Net sales are given to show that the figure represents the amount of money actually received after allowing for discounts and returned goods.

Net sales or gross revenues, you will note, is given before any kind of miscellaneous revenue that might have been received from investments, the sale of company property, tax refunds, or the like. A well-prepared income statement is always set up this way so that the stockholder can estimate the success of the company in fulfilling its major job of selling goods or service. If this were not so, you could not tell whether the company was really losing or making money on its operations, particularly over the last few years when tax rebates and other unusual things have often had great influence on final net income figures.

COST OF SALES

A general heading, *Cost of Sales, Expenses and Other Operating Charges* (item "b") is characteristic of a manufacturing company, but a utility company or railroad would call all of these things *operating expenses.*

The most important subdivision is *Cost of Goods Sold* (item "c"). Included under cost of goods sold are all of the expenses that go directly into the manufacture of the products the company sells -- raw materials, wages, freight, power, and rent. We have lumped these expenses together, as many companies do. Sometimes, however, you will find each item listed separately. Analyzing a detailed income account is a pretty technical operation and had best be left to the expert.

The ABC Manufacturing Company, Inc.
CONSOLIDATED INCOME AND EARNED SURPLUS
For the Year Ended December 31

Item			
a.	Sales		$10,000,000
b.	COST OF SALES, EXPENSES AND OTHER OPERATING CHARGES:		
c.	Cost of Goods Sold	$7,000,000	
d.	Selling, Administrative & Gen. Expenses	500,000	
e.	Depreciation	200,000	
f.	Maintenance and Repairs	400,000	
g.	Taxes (Other than Federal Inc. Taxes)	300,000	8,400,000
h.	NET PROFIT FROM OPERATIONS		$ 1,600,000
i.	OTHER INCOME:		
j.	Royalties and Dividends	$ 250,000	
k.	Interest	25,000	275,000
l.	TOTAL		$ 1,875,000
m.	INTEREST CHARGES:		
n.	Interest on Funded Debt	$ 70,000	
o.	Other Interest	20,000	90,000
p.	NET INCOME BEFORE PROVISION FOR FED. INCOME TAXES		$ 1,785,000
q.	PROVISION FOR FEDERAL INCOME TAXES		678,300
r.	NET INCOME		$ 1,106,700
s.	DIVIDENDS:		
t.	Preferred Stock - $5.00 Per Share	$ 50,000	
u.	Common Stock - $1.00 Per Share	400,000	
v.	PROVISION FOR CONTINGENCIES	200,000	650,000
w.	BALANCE CARRIED TO EARNED SURPLUS		$ 456,700
x.	EARNED SURPLUS – JANUARY 1		3,073,000
y.	EARNED SURPLUS – DECEMBER 31		$ 3,530,000

We have shown separately, opposite "d," the *Selling, Administrative and General Expenses* of the past year. Unfortunately, there is little uniformity among companies in their treatment of these important non-manufacturing costs. Our figure includes the expenses of management; that is, executive salaries and clerical costs; commissions and salaries paid to salesmen; advertising expenses, and the like.

Depreciation ("e") shows us the amount that the company transferred from income during the year to the depreciation reserve that we ran across before as item "11" on the balance sheet (page 2). Depreciation must be charged against income unless the company is going to live on its own fat, something that no company can do for long and stay out of bankruptcy.

MAINTENANCE

Maintenance and Repairs (item "f") represents the money spent to keep the plant in good operating order. For example, the truck that we mentioned under depreciation must be kept running day by day. The cost of new tires, recharging the battery, painting and mechanical repairs are all maintenance costs. Despite this day-to-day work on the truck, the company must still provide for the time when it wears out -- hence, the reserve for depreciation.

You can readily understand from your own experience the close connection between maintenance and depreciation. If you do not take good care of your own car, you will have to buy a new one sooner than you would had you maintained it well. Corporations face the same problem with all of their equipment. If they do not do a good job of maintenance, much more will have to be set aside for depreciation to replace the abused tools and property.

Taxes are always with us. A profitable company always pays at least two types of taxes. One group of taxes are paid without regard to profits, and include real estate taxes, excise taxes, social security, and the like (item "g"). As these payments are a direct part of the cost of doing business, they must be included before we can determine the *Net Profit From Operations* (item "h").

Net Profit from Operations (sometimes called *gross profit)* tells us what the company made from manufacturing and selling its products. It is an interesting figure to investors because it indicates .how efficiently and successfully the company operates in its primary purpose as a creator of wealth. As a glance at the income account will tell you, there are still several other items to be deducted before the stockholder can hope to get anything. You can also easily imagine that for many companies these other items may spell the difference between profit and loss. For these reasons, we use net profit from operations as an indicator of progress in manufacturing and merchandising efficiency, not as a judge of the investment quality of securities.

Miscellaneous Income not connected with the major purpose of the company is generally listed after net profit from operations. There are quite a number of ways that corporations increase their income, including interest and dividends on securities they own, fees for special services performed, royalties on patents they allow others to use, and tax refunds. Our income statement shows *Other Income* as item "i," under which is shown income from *Royalties and Dividends* (item "j"), and, as a separate entry, *Interest* (item "k") which the company received from its bond investments. The *Total* of other income (item t1t?) shows us how much The ABC Manufacturing Company received from so-called *outside activities.* Corporations with diversified interests often receive tremendous amounts of *other income.*

INTEREST CHARGES

There is one other class of expenses that must be deducted from our income before we can determine the base on which taxes are paid, and that is *Interest Charges* (item "m"). As our company has $2,000,000 worth of 3 1/2 per cent bonds outstanding, it will pay *Interest on Funded Debt* of $70,000 (item "n"). During the year, the company also borrowed money from the bank, on which it, of course, paid interest, shown as *Other Interest* (item "o").

Net Income Before Provision for Federal Income Taxes (item "p") is an interesting figure for historical comparison. It shows us how profitable the company was in all of its various operations. A comparison of this entry over a period of years will enable you to see how well the company had been doing as a business institution before the Government stepped in for its share of net earnings. Federal taxes have varied so much in recent years that earnings before taxes are often a real help in judging business progress.

A few paragraphs back we mentioned that a profitable corporation pays two general types of taxes. We have already discussed those that are paid without reference to profits. *Provision for Federal Income Taxes* (item "q") is ordinarily figured on the total income of the company after normal business expenses, and so appears on our income account below these charges. Bond interest, for example, as it is payment on a loan, is deducted beforehand. Preferred and common stock dividends, which are *profits* that go to owners of the company, come after all charges and taxes.

NET INCOME

After we have deducted all of our expenses and income taxes from total income, we get *Net Income* (item "r"). Net income is the most interesting figure of all to the investor. Net income is the amount available to pay dividends on the preferred and common stock. From the balance sheet, we have learned a good deal about the company's stability and soundness of structure; from net profit from operations, we judge whether the company is improving in industrial efficiency. Net income tells us whether the securities of the company are likely to be a profitable investment.

The figure given for a single year is not nearly all of the story, however. As we have noted before, the historical record is usually more important than the figure for any given year. This is just as true of net income as any other item. So many things change from year to year that care must be taken not to draw hasty conclusions. During the war, Excess Profits Taxes had a tremendous effect on the earnings of many companies. In the next few years, *carryback tax credits* allowed some companies to show a net profit despite the fact that they had operated at a loss. Even net income can be a misleading figure unless one examines it carefully. A rough and easy way of judging how *sound* a figure it is would be to compare it with previous years.

The investor in stocks has a vital interest in *Dividends* (item "s"). The first dividend that our company must pay is that on its *Preferred Stock* (item "t"). Some companies will even pay preferred dividends out of earned surplus accumulated in the past if the net income is not large enough, but such a company is skating on thin ice unless the situation is most unusual.

The directors of our company decided to pay dividends totaling $400,000 on the *Common Stock,* or $1 a share (item "u"). As we have noted before, the amount of dividends paid is not determined by net income, but by a decision of the stockholders' representatives - the company's directors. Common dividends, just like preferred dividends, can be paid out of surplus if there is little or no net income. Sometimes companies do this if they have a long history of regular payments and don't want to spoil the record because of some special temporary situation that caused them to lose money. This occurs even less frequently and is more *dangerous* than paying preferred dividends out of surplus.

It is much more common, on the contrary, to *plough earnings back into the business* -- a phrase you frequently see on the financial pages and in company reports. The directors of our typical company have decided to pay only $1 on the common stock, though net income would have permitted them to pay much more. They decided that the company should *save* the difference.

The next entry on our income account, *Provision for Contingencies* (item "v"), shows us where our reserve for contingencies arose. The treasurer of our typical company has put the provision for contingencies after dividends. However, you will discover, if you look at very many financial reports, that it is sometimes placed above net income.

All of the net income that was not paid out as dividends, or set aside for contingencies, is shown as *Balance Carried to Earned Surplus* (item "w"). In other words, it is kept in the business. In previous years, the company had also earned more than it paid out so it had already accumulated by the beginning of the year an earned surplus of $3,073,000 (item "x"). When we total the earned surplus accumulated during the year to that which the company had at the first of the year, we get the total earned surplus at the end' of the year (item "y"). You will notice that the total here is the same as that which we ran across on the balance sheet as item 27.

Not all companies combine their income and surplus account. When they do not, you will find that *balance carried to surplus will* be the last item on the income account. The statement of consolidated surplus would appear as a third section of the corporation's financial report. A separate surplus account might be used if the company shifted funds for reserves to surplus during the year or made any other major changes in its method of treating the surplus account.

ANALYZING THE INCOME ACCOUNT

The income account, like the balance sheet, will tell us a lot more if we make a few detailed comparisons. The size of the totals on an income account doesn't mean much by itself. A company can have hundreds of millions of dollars in net sales and be a very bad investment. On the other hand, even a very modest profit in round figures may make a security attractive if there are only a small number of shares outstanding.

Before you select a company for investment, you will want to know something of its *margin of profit,* and how this figure has changed over the years. Finding the margin of profit is very simple. We just divide the net profit from operations (item "h") by net sales (item "a"). The figure we get (0.16) shows us that the company make a profit of 16 per cent from operations. By itself, though, this is not very helpful. We can make it significant in two ways.

In the first place, we can compare it with the margin of profit in previous years, and, from this comparison, learn if the company excels other companies that do a similar type of business. If the margin of profit of our company is very low in comparison with other companies in the same field, it is an unhealthy sign. Naturally, if it is high, we have grounds to be optimistic.

Analysts also frequently use *operating ratio* for the same purpose. The operating ratio is the complement of the margin of profit. The margin of profit of our typical company is 16. The operating ratio is 84. You can find the operating ratio either by subtracting the margin of profit from 100 or dividing the total of operating costs ($8,400,000) by net sales ($10,000,000).

The margin of profit figure and the operating ratio, like all of those ratios we examined in connection with the balance sheet, give us general information about the company, help us judge its prospects for the future. All of these comparisons have significance for the long term as they tell us about the fundamental economic condition of the company. But you still have the right to ask: *"Are the securities good investments for me now?"*

Investors, as opposed to speculators, are primarily interested in two things. The first is safety for their capital and the second, regularity of income. They are also interested in the rate of return on their investment but, as you will see, the rate of return will be affected by the importance placed on safety and regularity. High income implies risk. Safety must be bought by accepting a lower return.

The safety of any security is determined primarily by the earnings of the company that are available to pay interest or dividends on the particular issue. Again, though, round dollar figures aren't of much help to us. What we want to know is the relationship between the total money available and the requirements for each of the securities issued by the company.

INTEREST COVERAGE

As the bonds of our company represent part of its debt, the first thing we want to know is how easily the company can pay the interest. From the income account we see that the company had total income of $1,875,000 (item "1"). The interest charge on our bonds each year is $70,000 (3 1/2 per cent of $2,000,000 - item 21 on the balance sheet). Dividing total income by bond interest charges ($1,875,000 by $70,000) shows us that the company earned its bond interest 26 times over. Even after income taxes, bond interest was earned 17 times, a method of testing employed by conservative analysts. Before an industrial bond should be considered a safe investment, most analysts say that the company should earn interest charges several times over, so our company has a wide margin of safety.

To calculate the *preferred dividend coverage* (i.e., the number of times preferred dividends were earned), we must use net income as our base, as Federal Income Taxes and all interest charges must be paid before anything is available for stockholders. As we have 10,000 shares of $100 par value of preferred stock which pays a dividend of 5 per cent, the total dividend requirement for the preferred stock is $50,000 (items 24 on the balance sheet and "t" on the income account).

EARNINGS PER COMMON SHARE

The buyer of common stocks is often more concerned with the earnings per share of his stock than he is with the dividend. It is usually earnings per share or, rather, prospective earnings per share, that influence stock market prices. Our income account does not show the earnings available for the common stock, so we must calculate it ourselves. It is net income less preferred dividends (items "r" - "t"), or $1,056,700. From the balance sheet, we know that there are 400,000 shares outstanding, so the company earned about $2.64 per share.

All of these ratios have been calculated for a single year. It cannot be emphasized too strongly, however, that the *record* is more important to the investor than the report of any single year. By all the tests we have employed, both the bonds and the preferred stock of our typical company appear to be very good investments,, if their market prices were not too high. The investor would want to look back, however, to determine whether the operations were reasonably typical of the company.

Bonds and preferred stocks that are very safe usually sell at pretty high prices, so the yield to the investor is small. For example, if our company has been showing about the same coverage on its preferred dividends for many years and there is good reason to believe that the future will be equally kind, the company would probably replace the old 5 per cent preferred with a new issue paying a lower rate, perhaps 4 per cent.

STOCK PRICES

As the common stock does not receive a guaranteed dividend, its market value is determined by a great variety of influences in addition to the present yield of the stock measured by its dividends. The stock market, by bringing together buyers and sellers from all over the world, reflects their composite judgment of the present and future value of the stock. We cannot attempt here to write a treatise on the stock market. There is one important ratio, however, that every common stock buyer considers. That is the ratio of earnings to market price.

The so-called *price-earnings ratio is* simply the earnings per share on the common stock divided into the market price. Our typical company earned $2.64 a common share in the year, If the stock were selling at $30 a share, its price-earnings ratio would be about 11.4. This is the basic figure that you would want to use in comparing the common stock of this particular company with other similar stocks.

IMPORTANT TERMS AND CONCEPTS

LIABILITIES
WHAT THE COMPANY OWES -- + RESERVES + SURPLUS + STOCKHOLDERS INTEREST IN THE COMPANY

ASSETS
WHAT THE COMPANY OWNS -- + WHAT IS OWED TO THE COMPANY

FIXED ASSETS
MACHINERY, EQUIPMENT, BUILDINGS, ETC.

EXAMPLES OF FIXED ASSETS
DESKS, TABLES, FILING CABINETS, BUILDINGS, LAND, TIMBERLAND, CARS AND TRUCKS, LOCOMOTIVES AND FREIGHT CARS, SHIPYARDS, OIL LANDS, ORE DEPOSITS, FOUNDRIES

EXAMPLES OF:

PREPAID EXPENSES
PREPAID INSURANCE, PREPAID RENT, PREPAID ROYALTIES AND PREPAID INTEREST

DEFERRED CHARGES
AMORTIZATION OF BOND DISCOUNT, ORGANIZATION EXPENSE, MOVING EXPENSES, DEVELOPMENT EXPENSES

ACCOUNTS PAYABLE
BILLS THE COMPANY OWES TO OTHERS

BONDHOLDERS ARE CREDITORS
BOND CERTIFICATES ARE IOU'S ISSUED BY A COMPANY BACKED BY A PLEDGE

BONDHOLDERS ARE OWNERS
A STOCK CERTIFICATE IS EVIDENCE OF THE SHAREHOLDER'S OWNERSHIP

EARNED SURPLUS
INCOME PLOWED BACK INTO THE BUSINESS

NET SALES
GROSS SALES MINUS DISCOUNTS AND RETURNED GOODS

NET INCOME
= TOTAL INCOME MINUS ALL EXPENSES AND INCOME TAXES

ANSWER SHEET

TEST NO. ______________ PART ______ TITLE OF POSITION ______________________________
(AS GIVEN IN EXAMINATION ANNOUNCEMENT - INCLUDE OPTION, IF ANY)

PLACE OF EXAMINATION ______________________________ ______________ DATE ______________
(CITY OR TOWN) (STATE)

RATING

USE THE SPECIAL PENCIL. MAKE GLOSSY BLACK MARKS.

1	A	B	C	D	E	26	A	B	C	D	E	51	A	B	C	D	E	76	A	B	C	D	E	101	A	B	C	D	E
2	A	B	C	D	E	27	A	B	C	D	E	52	A	B	C	D	E	77	A	B	C	D	E	102	A	B	C	D	E
3	A	B	C	D	E	28	A	B	C	D	E	53	A	B	C	D	E	78	A	B	C	D	E	103	A	B	C	D	E
4	A	B	C	D	E	29	A	B	C	D	E	54	A	B	C	D	E	79	A	B	C	D	E	104	A	B	C	D	E
5	A	B	C	D	E	30	A	B	C	D	E	55	A	B	C	D	E	80	A	B	C	D	E	105	A	B	C	D	E
6	A	B	C	D	E	31	A	B	C	D	E	56	A	B	C	D	E	81	A	B	C	D	E	106	A	B	C	D	E
7	A	B	C	D	E	32	A	B	C	D	E	57	A	B	C	D	E	82	A	B	C	D	E	107	A	B	C	D	E
8	A	B	C	D	E	33	A	B	C	D	E	58	A	B	C	D	E	83	A	B	C	D	E	108	A	B	C	D	E
9	A	B	C	D	E	34	A	B	C	D	E	59	A	B	C	D	E	84	A	B	C	D	E	109	A	B	C	D	E
10	A	B	C	D	E	35	A	B	C	D	E	60	A	B	C	D	E	85	A	B	C	D	E	110	A	B	C	D	E

Make only ONE mark for each answer. Additional and stray marks may be counted as mistakes. In making corrections, erase errors COMPLETELY.

11	A	B	C	D	E	36	A	B	C	D	E	61	A	B	C	D	E	86	A	B	C	D	E	111	A	B	C	D	E
12	A	B	C	D	E	37	A	B	C	D	E	62	A	B	C	D	E	87	A	B	C	D	E	112	A	B	C	D	E
13	A	B	C	D	E	38	A	B	C	D	E	63	A	B	C	D	E	88	A	B	C	D	E	113	A	B	C	D	E
14	A	B	C	D	E	39	A	B	C	D	E	64	A	B	C	D	E	89	A	B	C	D	E	114	A	B	C	D	E
15	A	B	C	D	E	40	A	B	C	D	E	65	A	B	C	D	E	90	A	B	C	D	E	115	A	B	C	D	E
16	A	B	C	D	E	41	A	B	C	D	E	66	A	B	C	D	E	91	A	B	C	D	E	116	A	B	C	D	E
17	A	B	C	D	E	42	A	B	C	D	E	67	A	B	C	D	E	92	A	B	C	D	E	117	A	B	C	D	E
18	A	B	C	D	E	43	A	B	C	D	E	68	A	B	C	D	E	93	A	B	C	D	E	118	A	B	C	D	E
19	A	B	C	D	E	44	A	B	C	D	E	69	A	B	C	D	E	94	A	B	C	D	E	119	A	B	C	D	E
20	A	B	C	D	E	45	A	B	C	D	E	70	A	B	C	D	E	95	A	B	C	D	E	120	A	B	C	D	E
21	A	B	C	D	E	46	A	B	C	D	E	71	A	B	C	D	E	96	A	B	C	D	E	121	A	B	C	D	E
22	A	B	C	D	E	47	A	B	C	D	E	72	A	B	C	D	E	97	A	B	C	D	E	122	A	B	C	D	E
23	A	B	C	D	E	48	A	B	C	D	E	73	A	B	C	D	E	98	A	B	C	D	E	123	A	B	C	D	E
24	A	B	C	D	E	49	A	B	C	D	E	74	A	B	C	D	E	99	A	B	C	D	E	124	A	B	C	D	E
25	A	B	C	D	E	50	A	B	C	D	E	75	A	B	C	D	E	100	A	B	C	D	E	125	A	B	C	D	E

SEP 2013

ANSWER SHEET

TEST NO. ______________ PART ______ TITLE OF POSITION ______________________________
(AS GIVEN IN EXAMINATION ANNOUNCEMENT - INCLUDE OPTION, IF ANY)

PLACE OF EXAMINATION ______________________________ DATE ______
(CITY OR TOWN) (STATE)

RATING

USE THE SPECIAL PENCIL. MAKE GLOSSY BLACK MARKS.

1 A B C D E	26 A B C D E	51 A B C D E	76 A B C D E	101 A B C D E
2 A B C D E	27 A B C D E	52 A B C D E	77 A B C D E	102 A B C D E
3 A B C D E	28 A B C D E	53 A B C D E	78 A B C D E	103 A B C D E
4 A B C D E	29 A B C D E	54 A B C D E	79 A B C D E	104 A B C D E
5 A B C D E	30 A B C D E	55 A B C D E	80 A B C D E	105 A B C D E
6 A B C D E	31 A B C D E	56 A B C D E	81 A B C D E	106 A B C D E
7 A B C D E	32 A B C D E	57 A B C D E	82 A B C D E	107 A B C D E
8 A B C D E	33 A B C D E	58 A B C D E	83 A B C D E	108 A B C D E
9 A B C D E	34 A B C D E	59 A B C D E	84 A B C D E	109 A B C D E
10 A B C D E	35 A B C D E	60 A B C D E	85 A B C D E	110 A B C D E

Make only ONE mark for each answer. Additional and stray marks may be counted as mistakes. In making corrections, erase errors COMPLETELY.

11 A B C D E	36 A B C D E	61 A B C D E	86 A B C D E	111 A B C D E
12 A B C D E	37 A B C D E	62 A B C D E	87 A B C D E	112 A B C D E
13 A B C D E	38 A B C D E	63 A B C D E	88 A B C D E	113 A B C D E
14 A B C D E	39 A B C D E	64 A B C D E	89 A B C D E	114 A B C D E
15 A B C D E	40 A B C D E	65 A B C D E	90 A B C D E	115 A B C D E
16 A B C D E	41 A B C D E	66 A B C D E	91 A B C D E	116 A B C D E
17 A B C D E	42 A B C D E	67 A B C D E	92 A B C D E	117 A B C D E
18 A B C D E	43 A B C D E	68 A B C D E	93 A B C D E	118 A B C D E
19 A B C D E	44 A B C D E	69 A B C D E	94 A B C D E	119 A B C D E
20 A B C D E	45 A B C D E	70 A B C D E	95 A B C D E	120 A B C D E
21 A B C D E	46 A B C D E	71 A B C D E	96 A B C D E	121 A B C D E
22 A B C D E	47 A B C D E	72 A B C D E	97 A B C D E	122 A B C D E
23 A B C D E	48 A B C D E	73 A B C D E	98 A B C D E	123 A B C D E
24 A B C D E	49 A B C D E	74 A B C D E	99 A B C D E	124 A B C D E
25 A B C D E	50 A B C D E	75 A B C D E	100 A B C D E	125 A B C D E